Gardening like a
NINJA

A GUIDE TO SNEAKING DELICIOUS EDIBLES INTO YOUR LANDSCAPE

Praise for Gardening like a Ninja

"Grow food without sacrificing interest and beauty with Angela England's tried-and-true edible landscaping advice."

"Angela England does it again. With her kind heart, knowledgeable guidance, and can-do attitude England takes us from a place of peeking-around-the-corner-curiosity to hands-on-our-hips-getting-the-job-done-and-loving-it with *Gardening Like a Ninja*.

"From understanding basic landscape design, to creating interest throughout the season, to understanding how hardscaping elements can work for your landscape, Angela England's *Gardening Like a Ninja* brings it."

"With so many people turning to gardening as a source of food and a way to have certainty on how your family is fed, Gardening Like a Ninja couldn't have had better timing. Angela England is the person I go to for advice on anything related to growing food on my property. And in California, where I live, with very limited water resources, so many people have turned to front yard gardening to replace grass and become more efficient with their use of space on their property. Why waste your water on grass when it doesn't produce anything? This book's time has come, and I'm very happy to recommend it to the Mamavation audience.

Gardening like a
NINJA

A GUIDE TO SNEAKING DELICIOUS EDIBLES INTO YOUR LANDSCAPE

ANGELA ENGLAND
Illustrated by Wendy Piersall

HOBBLE CREEK PRESS | AN IMPRINT OF CEDAR FORT, INC. | SPRINGVILLE, UTAH

The opinions and views expressed herein belong solely to the author and do not necessarily represent the opinions or views of Cedar Fort, Inc. Permission for the use of sources, graphics, and photos is also solely the responsibility of the author.

ISBN 978-1-4621-1808-3

Published by Hobble Creek Press, an imprint of Cedar Fort, Inc.
2373 W. 700 S., Springville, UT, 84663
Distributed by Cedar Fort, Inc., www.cedarfort.com

LIBRARY OF CONGRESS CATALOGING-IN-PUBLICATION DATA

England, Angela, author.
Gardening like a ninja / Angela England.
    pages cm
    ISBN 978-1-4621-1808-3 (layflat binding : alk. paper)
    1. Edible landscaping. I. Title.
    SB475.9.E35E54 2015
    635'.1--dc23

                    2015033398

Cover and page design M. Shaun McMurdie
Cover design © 2016 Cedar Fort, Inc.
Edited by Melissa J. Caldwell and Justin Greer

Printed in China

10   9   8   7   6   5   4   3   2   1

Printed on acid-free paper.

Dedication

I dedicate this book to my husband, Sidney England,
as we make our new house a delightful home.

Never boring.

Contents

Foreword

A garden is far more than *just* a garden. No matter the square footage you have to plant in, it is possible to grow something simple and beautiful. Ornamental edible vegetables and herbs, in particular, deliver something far vaster than a flavorful bite and the foliage of ornamental edibles can be magnificent in the landscape.

Growing in itself is therapeutic. Placing our hands in the soil is like a deep breath. We can feel the stress melt away as we plant, water, and tend the flowers and edibles that make up our balcony or patio gardens. We connect on a deep level with the beautiful smells in an herbal garden, the bold colors of a mixed edible border, or the tastes of a freshly picked herb. This is the thing about gardening—it is a soul-relieving practice of the heart, which breathes pain and sorrow in and exhales happiness. Landscaping with edibles extends this practice so that it is possible to walk by hedgerows of herbs and have gorgeous groundcovers that can be picked and cooked at your pleasure.

Ornamental edibles are most profound because they are specifically useful. While beautiful, most ornamental edibles (such as mustard, kale, Swiss chard, blood beets, and the like) are also filled with an overabundance of vitamins and minerals. This gives a justification for landscaping seed money because ornamental edibles provide more than beauty and are meant for a higher goal: your dinner table.

Gardening Like a Ninja: A Guide to Sneaking Delicious Edibles into Your Landscape is connecting that passion for beauty with the increasing demand for freshly grown organic vegetables. Knowing what fertilizers and soil amendments your landscape has means you have an intrinsic control over the chemical levels of foods that go into the diet of your family. Because a garden is far more than just a garden in the landscape; it is your health and happiness.

— Shawna Coronado, www.shawnacoronado.com

Preface

When I wrote *Backyard Farming on an Acre (More or Less)*, I was overwhelmed and humbled by the responses I got from readers who were making incredible strides in their journey toward greater self-sufficiency. But sometimes, someone would ask me what they could do if they lived in an area that wouldn't allow a large vegetable garden, or if they had a fussy HOA and picky neighbors. That's what this book is intended to answer—a way for anyone, anywhere, to create a beautifully landscape garden that would provide for them.

Right before I agreed to tackle this book, I moved to a new house. It suits our family better in many regards but had no landscaping whatsoever. Throughout this book, you will see original garden designs that are based on the dimensions of my actual home and the space I have to work with. You'll see the thought process I use in overcoming challenges, like a shady entryway or the need for a low-maintenance garden near the mailbox.

My hope is that you'll be able to use those ideas and apply them to your own homes and situations. Part One of this book will show you the basics of landscape design and successful gardening. It will set a firm foundation of basic knowledge for you that you can then apply to your own unique circumstances.

Part Two of this book includes original landscape designs created just for this project. You'll find all aspects of the home covered, as well as many gardening challenges such as concrete patios and small side yards. These original designs aren't meant for you to duplicate exactly, but rather for you to use and adapt with your own style, color preferences, and favorite edibles.

Which leads me to Part Three—the plant recommendations. In these chapters you'll find detailed growing guides of several types of plants. Trees, shrubs, vines, ground covers, perennials, and annuals are all covered. There are detailed explanations of how to grow them, how to harvest them, and how to use them, and there are specific cultivars that have something special to offer a gardening ninja.

Taken together, these chapters will give you everything you need to transform your home's landscaping from Stepford-wife-boring to a unique and stunning bounty. Join me as I undertake remaking my home's gardens, and see other readers as they embark on their journey as well.

Find all the ways to connect with us and continue your journey at http://UntrainedHousewife.com/GardeningLikeANinja.

Acknowledgments

I am so grateful to everyone who made this book a possibility. First, to my family. To my husband, who has never failed to jump into new adventures with me. Thank you for always having my back—and knowing where my keys are. To my five children, who let me sleep an extra fifteen minutes when I'd been up late writing and woke me with fresh-brewed coffee. Thank you for teaching me to be brave.

To my mother-in-law, who was the force of sanity behind this project and truly made it possible. Thank you for wrestling the minions so I could shut myself up with my computer for more than minutes at a time. To my parents, who taught me to pursue my interests. Thank you for teaching me to learn.

Second, to my community. To my church family, who inspires and encourages me. I wouldn't be who I am without you. To the ladies at the library who gave me fast Internet and let me stay after hours. This book wouldn't exist without your help.

To the garden writers who encourage me and teach me from their brilliant writing every year. You inspire me. To the members of Homestead Bloggers Network. Your wisdom and loyalty mean the world to me.

To my colleagues on this book project. To Wendy, for taking my original sketches and mad ramblings and bringing them to life—you made my visions take shape. To Ashley, Melissa, and Justin, for tracking down all the stray commas and run-away sentence fragments. To Shaun, for crafting the many pieces into a lovely and beautiful whole. This project is better because of your involvement.

Last, to my friends. To all who called to check on me, sent me food, wished me well, made coffee, or forgave a delayed reply. You bless me and I'm a better person for having you in my life.

PART I

Why Sneak Edibles Into Your Landscape?

Gardening like a ninja is about transforming your landscape from boring and useless eye candy into a vibrant and exciting bounty. The best part is that your neighbors will never know the difference. When you sneak these amazing plants into your landscape, in a way that defies logic, you'll have all the benefits of traditional landscaping curb appeal, as well as saving yourself a trip to the Farmer's Market on occasion. You can have it all!

What Is Edible Landscaping?

Edible landscaping is a little bit of a buzzword right now, and there are several ways you can define it. For me, it means presenting your edible foods within the framework of typical home landscaping and making it look attractive while also being productive! As a result of using dual-purpose plants, you reap myriad benefits.

We recently moved to a home that has lots of potential but very little landscaping. In

Come see some of the plans I have in place, and begin to dream about what you can do with your own unique spaces!

BENEFITS OF GARDENING LIKE A NINJA

Have you ever noticed in the movies that ninjas are both smart and sneaky? They

Harvesting delicious edibles right from your own yard does not have to ruin the look of your landscape. You CAN have both! Photo courtesy of Michele Bastian.

In the 1940s, many Americans planted edibles in their urban and suburban homes, spurred by the Victory Garden Eleanor Roosevelt planted at the White House. These efforts were highly successful with some accounts suggesting that 40 percent of the produce consumed by American during this time had been grown at home.

many ways, this is a good thing because then I won't feel guilty ripping out ornamental plants to replace them with edibles. I will start from scratch, make careful plans, and then plant exactly what we want and need.

don't waste movements but work efficiently and wisely. And you don't always see them coming! That's what edible landscaping is like—no wasted moves (or in this case plants) and no one realizes what

"The best time to plant a tree was twenty years ago. The second best time is today." —Chinese Proverb

you're doing at first glance. It looks like a beautifully designed garden and then it's only at second glance that you realize it's also incredibly productive.

There are so many benefits of edible landscaping that I'm always a little surprised more home owners don't do it. Yes, you have to be just a little more strategic with your planning up front; however, once you've established your garden spaces, there's usually not an overwhelming amount of maintenance. And the benefits far outweigh any temporary hassle.

PRODUCING HOMEGROWN FOOD

Of course, one of the main benefits of edible landscaping is just that—the edibles! The ability to produce your own food items, right in your own yard, bring an immeasurable sense of satisfaction. And you do not have to anger your HOA or sacrifice curb appeal to achieve a landscape both beautiful and productive if you give some thought to the plants you choose and how you use them.

This lovely border is a great example of gardening like a ninja. It's chock full of edibles, herbs, and pollinators! The accent trees are peaches, the understory has fruitful shrubs and herbaceous perennials, while ground covers include annual vegetables. Brilliant! Photo courtesy of M. Williams, founder of A Moveable Garden.

These Cajun Belle peppers are just the beginning of what's available from an edible landscape—right out your front door! Photo courtesy of All-America Selections.

Growing your own food will give you the opportunity to provide your family with healthier alternatives to traditional store-bought produce. Of course we all know that we should eat more herbs, fruits, and vegetables. When it's literally staring you in the face as you walk outside to check the mail, it's harder to ignore. Especially for families.

If you have kids, the principles from Gardening Like a Ninja will appeal to them a great deal. Most parents find their children are much more agreeable to eating vegetables from their yard. Partly because they have a pride in having been part of the process. But perhaps also because of the amazing flavor difference!

All the benefits you would think of when it comes to growing fruits, herbs, and vegetables in general (cost, nutrition, family-togetherness, and so on) all apply to edible landscaping as well. The improved ecological impact of the home is also something worth mentioning. The primary difference, however, is that your edibles aren't laid out in the tradition fenced-in-rows of a typical vegetable garden.

FOCUS ON BEAUTY IS EQUALLY IMPORTANT

With edible landscaping a home owner can float under the radar of an over-eager HOA because there is as much an emphasis on form as function. Yes, you are using edible plants, but only such plants as lend themselves to an overall attractive landscape design as a whole. The goal is to mimic traditional landscape techniques with plants that are practical. And there are so many!

Later chapters of this book will show you not only the basics of landscape design (what draws the eye and creates impressive effects in the home garden) but also which plants are naturally well-suited to an edible landscape plan. We will also discuss each plant's unique requirements so you can be sure to place similarly suited plants together. This will give you the foundation for creating beautiful landscaping around your home that will include delicious fruits, herbs, and vegetables at the same time.

SAVING MONEY WITH HOMEGROWN EDIBLES

I'd be remiss if I didn't mention cost as a benefit to growing your own edibles. Fresh fruits and vegetables can be pricy, and fresh herbs even more so. For example, in our local grocery store a fresh sprig of basil costs $3.50, and I get maybe a dozen or so leaves total. But I can take a $1-package of seeds and have all the basil I can eat, and the seed packet usually lasts more than one year! That's a huge savings in just one plant.

Don't have room for a full-sized shade tree on your property? Don't worry. I will share some of the smaller, fruiting trees, shrubs, and vines in future chapters.

Organic food can be even more expensive to pick up at the grocery store. So adding a layer of edible plants to your landscaping can provide a savings on your grocery budget. If you save even a handful of shopping trips throughout the year, it will add up. Especially when you consider you're using areas of your property that you would want to landscape or plant anyway! You sneaky ninja, you.

When I was researching my first book, *Backyard Farming on an Acre (More or Less)*, I learned that studies show, on average, for every dollar invested in an edible gardening area, there is six dollars worth of vegetables harvested. What a great return on investment!

"Growing food is like printing your own money." —Ron Finley

EXAMPLES OF EDIBLE LANDSCAPING IN ACTION

Wondering what it looks like? Here are some success stories of how others have used edible landscaping techniques with great results in their own home situations.

PRODUCTIVE SHADE TREE IN TEXAS

Our first home in West Texas had a fabulous example of edible landscaping in action. Most properties in this town had large shade trees on the property to help buffer against the pounding sun. Common shade trees are oak, magnolia, or in the South, catalpa trees. There's nothing wrong with any of those trees, per se, but they do not provide edible fruits like other trees selections would.

This property has a huge pecan tree on the side yard space. Its spreading branches shade the home all summer long. And, come fall, a bounty of nuts can be harvested right off the driveway! We usually harvested enough pecans for two or three pies per year from a space that could have otherwise been filled with an unproductive landscaping tree.

Some of my favorite full-sized shade trees to consider for edible landscaping are hickory, maple, chestnut, pecan, and walnut. These and other trees are discussed in Chapter 6 in more detail.

FRONT WALKWAY AND ENTRYWAY GARDEN

My friend Alexis has a full-sun front entry and took great care in the design of her entryway. I'm excited to share her example here as an inspiration of what you can do to transform your home. When they got the house, it was a typical suburban home.

Here Alexis describes how she transformed the look of the entryway border. She also describes how they prepared the soil to transform the lawn into an edible oasis.

Edible landscaping doesn't have to be overly complicated, and you can start slowly. It's never easy trying something new, but the rewards are so great. And you are not alone! The rest of this book is dedicated to helping you walk through this process, and you can join the Edible Landscaping Guide group on Facebook at www.facebook .com/groups/EdibleLandscapingGuide/ and see additional resources at UntrainedHousewife.com/GardeningLike ANinja.

In Chapter 2 we'll review the basics of landscape design principles. In Chapter 3, we'll look at how to garden anything. And then in Part 2 we'll introduce some original garden design ideas that will help you understand how to create your own designs. Finally, in Part 3, you will find growing guides that highlight not only great plants for edible landscape designs but also specific cultivars that have more landscape interest or more disease resistant.

BEFORE — Beautiful brick home with an utterly boring and non-useful walkway. The entryway is similar to all the other homes in the neighborhood. Photo courtesy of Alexis Watters, founder of BeanandBee.com.

Alexis Watters
Texas, Zone 8b

Edible Entryway and Foundation Border

About the borders: They are mostly all edible. Purple and silver sage, several varieties of lavender, and oregano are evergreen in my zone and provide color and structure all year. Garlic chives, echinacea, chicory, and others come in and out of season. Frog fruit, a Texas native, works as a living mulch and its tiny blooms attract many pollinators. Roses and a peach tree provide focal points.

I thought a lot about the look of the front yard edible landscaping because I wanted to show that growing food and having a beautiful yard don't have to be two separate endeavors. I limited the color palate to purples and silvers/ whites, with pops of contrast, like the yellow roses.

We replaced the standard walkway with a native limestone flagstone path. Creeping thyme and native frog fruit are starting to fill in the cracks between the stones. I love the English cottage garden style, but the central Texas Hill Country climate and soil don't generally lend themselves to the classic plants used.

I am in zone 8b and live in a bioregion that is known for long, hot summers and little topsoil. Soil-building is always on the agenda. I use a lot of coffee grounds, newspaper, and compost to start the beds and then top dress with

AFTER — The entryway is now a lush, edible bounty with beautiful layers of trees, shrubs, perennials, annuals, and ground covers. The remake of the pathway makes it much more inviting and complements the style well. Photo courtesy of Alexis Watters, founder of BeanandBee.com.

more compost and mulch twice a year. After the grass is removed, I try not to disturb the soil so a healthy soil web develops.

To get the romantic cottage garden look, I copied key elements like stone paths, roses, and the "overflowing" borders. I just put an edible (and Texas) twist on it.

We love having edibles right outside the front door. We use the fresh herbs for cooking almost daily. (Pork chops in a sage and brown butter sauce are a family favorite.) The kids check for berries every time we head out to the car. I put borage blossoms on their chicken nuggets to make them laugh. The thornless

blackberries are in their first year in this location and produced a few handfuls of tart fruit in late spring. I hope the harvest will improve in both quantity and flavor as the plants mature.

We only started this transformation two years ago. The plan is to expand it a little more every fall until there is only one small patch of grass left under the big shade tree. The herbs are the most productive right now. I hope in time the berries and peaches give us a bigger harvest. In the future I plan on adding a fig tree, pomegranate tree, and bay bush.

Mastering Landscape Design Elements

2

Edible landscaping doesn't change the basics of landscape design. Instead when you create an edible landscape, you're just transforming your beautiful landscape design to something that will include function as well as form. Understanding the basics of good landscaping design principles will equip you to "beat the

FOUR SEASONS OF INTEREST

One of the biggest mistakes I see in home landscapes—and, really, one of the hardest things to overcome as a gardener—is a lack of interest through multiple seasons. This can be so challenging!

This gorgeous landscape design looks beautiful with this home's New England style and yet is filled with many herbs and edibles. Photo courtesy of Liz West.

"A gardener's work is never at an end; it begins with the year and continues to the next."

—John Evelyn

HOA" and increase curb appeal, even while producing a bountiful garden. You truly can have both.

But first, here are some of the basic design elements to keep in mind when considering how to transform your landscape design.

Late spring/early summer is so easy. Everything is green. It seems like everything is flowering. It's certainly a time of immense growth. But what about midwinter in the landscape? A well-designed landscape should include

HARDSCAPING—the hardscaping of your landscape designs are those elements which are more or less permanent. Things like fences, arbors, trellises, porches, and so on would all be considered hardscape elements.

something interesting through multiple seasons. Let's talk about what can be done through each season of the landscape.

WINTER INTEREST IN THE LANDSCAPE

During the winter you notice more about the hardscaping and general design of your landscaping. This is great time to notice holes and make plans for next year. It's also a great time to take pleasure in the simple, small delights. Creating winter interest in the garden can be done through a variety of ways.

Hardscaping

Hardscaping elements take center stage during the winter. While during the summer months that wooden fence is merely a backdrop for the climbing pole beans and squash vines, in the winter it

These Echinacea stand out against the solid wood fence behind them. Attractive hardscaping elements like this will add to the landscape. Photo courtesy of Patrick Standish; Aurora, Colorado.

is the main focus. Suddenly the distressed staining or cool metal finials are what catches the eye.

Fences can be a great place to add eye-catching details, metal pieces, wall art, repurposed trellising, or other ornamental and useful elements. Other hardscape elements to pay attention to include pathways, gazebos or porches, large containers or raised beds, furniture pieces, and anything else that is permanent or semipermanent. Increase the curb appeal by making these cohesive in appearance with added and unexpected details.

This red thyme is covered in frost but holds its color through winter. Evergreen color is just one way to add winter interest. Photo courtesy of M. Williams, founder of A Moveable Garden.

Witch hazel has gorgeous yellow flowers that seem to glow in the winter sun. A great way to add color to the landscape before spring arrives. Photo courtesy of Missouri Botanical Garden.

Plants with Winter Berries and Seed Heads

Some plants in the landscape have attractive berries or seed heads on them that look good during the winter months. These include some hollies, beautyberries, hydrangeas, some grasses, and sedums. These stems, seeds, and pops of color add architectural elements to the garden landscape even during the winter when little else in growing.

Winter Flowers

Don't think that just because it is winter you can't enjoy blooms. I like to include ornamental plants that will have winter color in my landscapes, so there's a year-round appeal. Of course my focus is on edibles, but sometimes a well-placed ornamental is exactly what you need. Some of these amazing plants include witch hazel shrubs, hellebores (also called the Christmas Rose), and snow drops.

I usually mentally categorize plants like red-stemmed dogwoods into this section as well since they add attractive red coloring throughout the winter months in the form of red twigs. Color is color, right?

Evergreen Plants

Evergreen plants have a great purpose to an overall landscape design. They provide a strong foundation during the winter

Fruit trees and spring bulbs are a classic combination for early spring color. Photo by Amanda Attarian, courtesy of Missouri Botanical Garden.

"When the world wearies and society fails to satisfy, there is always a garden." —Minnie Aumonier

Lettuces and other cool-season greens can have really attractive foliage colors and contrast. Don't overlook these in the edible landscape. Photo courtesy of M. Williams, founder of A Moveable Garden.

Leafy Edibles and Greens

Spring is when leafy herbs take off—all the mesclun mixes, lettuces, and other greens like spinach or mustard. Lettuces and other similar plants can take the place of many edging annuals in the traditional landscape.

Instead of planting a ground cover of vinca vine or impatiens, sow seeds for a colorful lettuce blend and Swiss chard. You get the same green foil under and around larger plants, but you can actually walk through the garden harvesting the largest leaves as you go, and end up back at the house with a salad's worth for dinner.

One thing to keep in mind with a technique like this is that lettuce will give up and "bolt" after so many weeks. So every couple of weeks I mercilessly uproot an entire plant and replant a couple seeds in it's place. This keeps the border full since there are no large empty spots all at once.

At any given time, about a quarter of the greens in the bed or flower border are newly planted, a quarter are a week or two old, a quarter are maturing, and a quarter are ready to be harvested. By keeping the rotation going, it never takes more than a couple minutes each week for a bountiful salad-on-demand for my family supper table.

Spring-Blooming Bulbs

I do understand that most of the bulbs people think of in the spring aren't edible plants, but, wow, do they look amazing in a mixed border. I love tucking spring-blooming bulbs around the planting holes

BOLT—When lettuce bolts, it shoots a large flowering stalk upward from the center of the plant in order to begin producing seed. This process turns the leaves bitter. For purely edible considerations, the plant can be dug up and discarded as soon as this begins happening.

TIP!—Toss any extra plants you uproot into the compost bin. That way you aren't wasting the energy and nutrients that grew the plant; you're just repurposing and feeding it back into the garden in a few weeks.

when nothing else is green and act as a great backdrop to other plants during the other seasons. I would include these useful plants in an edible landscape because they provide evergreen or semi-evergreen color. Evergreen plants include two of my favorite garden herbs: rosemary and thyme.

These techniques blend all together to provide an overall strategy for creating winter interest during a time of the year when most people don't think about their gardens. Taking a bit of time to keep winter in mind during your planning phases can make a huge difference in providing a year-round landscape design.

SPRING IN THE LANDSCAPE

Spring eases in from late-winter snowdrops and crocuses to other flowering bulbs like tulips and iris. From there, the sky is the limit as annuals and fruit trees burst into bloom so they can begin the task of producing seed. Many perennials will lag behind a few weeks, but there's still a riot of color to enjoy in the spring garden.

of my larger perennials and shrubs when I'm planting.

They don't take up very much room and bloom before the other plants are growing. By the time the bulbs bloom and are dying off, the larger perennials or shrubs are leafing out and help to hide the yellowing foliage of the bulbs. To me there is little sacrificed for a fabulous and colorful gain.

Having said that, there actually are spring blooming bulbs that will produce edibles for you! In fact, in the United States some of these forgotten wild bulbs were an important staple in Native American and early American pioneer diets. For example, the blue camas (*Camassia esculenta*) have gorgeous blue flower spikes starting mid-spring. By the time blooms end in summer, the onion-like bulbs are ready to be harvested.

Annuals for Quick Color

A common trend in spring is to plant flats of annuals to create instant pops of color in your landscape design. With edible landscaping in mind, I try to have seeds started ahead of time to be ready to set out. When I forget or am unable to do that, I will focus my annual selection on plants that can be useful as well as beautiful.

Many garden centers sell herbs. Some of these herbs have gorgeous foliage like mint, basil, dill, and cilantro. Others have early but edible flowers like nasturtiums, violets, and pansies. Popping these colorful annuals into the landscape will fill in gaps with easy accent colors.

Fruit Tree Flowers

A common sight along many roadways during the spring weeks are gorgeous drifts of blooms from ornamental pears and other sterile fruit trees. I would contend that edible fruit trees have just as lovely flowers and can produce fabulous fruit to boot. Making a simple switch from purely ornamental crab apples to dwarf-but-true apples, for example, is a simple way to keep the best of both worlds.

Favorite fruit trees with amazing spring flowers in my area of the world are peaches, plums, cherries, and pears. Your area may support other types of trees, such as apple, with better success.

The spring flowers of fruit trees are so lovely—usually in shades of white or pink. Every landscape needs a gorgeous spring-blooming tree. Photo courtesy of Liz West.

Edible Annual Plants for Quick Color

Colorful lettuces

Nasturtiums

Primroses

Violets

Pansies

Cabbage

Peas

Swiss Chard

Primroses are an edible, colorful delight in early spring. Photo courtesy of Alfred Diem.

Edible Plants with Summer Flowers

Sage

Lavender

Basil

Hyssop

Bee Balm

Borage

Squash Blossoms

Chives

Cilantro

Dill

I recommend checking out Chapter 6 about fruits for growing details about the type of fruit that interests you. Another great place to get localized information is your county extension office.

Spring is the time for taking your winter planning and scheming and dreaming and hoping and making things happen.

SUMMER LANDSCAPE INTEREST

Capturing the eye in the summer isn't difficult. Many plants are in full bloom. Others are completely leafed out, and everything looks amazing. For many gardeners this can be a favorite time of year. In the summer, there is always something to harvest and nibble on as you wander through your garden.

This lovely summer border captures the eye with contrasts of shape and color.

Foliage Contrast

While we will discuss texture later on in this chapter, summer is the time of year when everything is leafed out, so the contrast of color and foliage type is most noticeable. This is where you'll want to have a discerning eye for the colors of the leaves. Sometimes by placing a plant with a specific type of foliage, say bright chartreuse, in front of some plants with a different color, say deep purple or bronze, you enhance the appearance of both plants.

I also love to consider the contrast between fine-cut foliage, like that of dill or rosemary, with broader leaves, like sweet basil or Swiss chard. Keep in mind that having an entire row of plants with a similar style of leaves will be more formal and uniform with fewer places to draw the eye or provide interest.

The summer is pretty easy for gardeners because flowers and fruit and beautiful plants abound. For me the toughest challenge isn't growing plants, but weeding out the plants I don't want growing. Keeping up with the harvests and making time to put up the extra food that is available makes me grateful for the longer days!

FALL LANDSCAPE INTEREST

When summer begins to shift into the fall season, we see a change in the landscape yet again. Perennial flowers take over as late-summer and autumn blooming plants shift into high gear. There's a shift in size and color that is a preparation for winter.

Some plants in the landscape create interest by producing nuts or large fruits. Deciduous shade trees that produce nuts are coming into season as hickory nuts, walnuts, pecans, and chestnuts all begin to

Edible Plants with Fall Interest

Blueberry

Cranberry

Pecan

Pine (Edible Nuts)

Beech

Rose Hips

Persimmon

Goldenrod

Serviceberry

Current

Many deciduous trees will put on a fall show with stunning foliage colors in the fall. These dogwoods are a lovely understory level plant that can add great interest year round. Photo courtesy of Sue St. Jean, founder of LessNoise-MoreGreen.com.

ripen. In fact, it can be easy to plant a nut tree in place of other common shade trees like oak or magnolia.

The other thing to think about in the fall is the potential for colorful foliage. Consider that not just trees but many shrubs can have brightly colored fall foliage as well. Reds, yellows, oranges, and everything in between is possible depending on the plant and climate. For example some blueberry plants turn red in autumn making them a double-duty plant in the edible landscape.

USING THE SENSES— TEXTURE AND FRAGRANCE

Using multiple senses in the edible landscaping is worth considering as you build your edible garden design. Texture and fragrance are both elements that can often be overlooked but will add incredible dimensions to your landscape, inviting you to lin-

ger and to literally stop and smell the roses. Sit at the steps with a cup of coffee or hot chocolate and touch a fuzzy sage leaf and feel the prickly fun of rosemary. An edible landscape should encourage exploration and delight the senses. All of them.

TEXTURE

The texture of foliage is both physical and visual. Visually, when you see a broad, green leaf like large-leaved Swiss chard it creates a wide swath of color. Fine-cut foliage like dill or fennel is a great example of pretty foliage that creates a lacy effect. Combined, they enhance the contrast between the two in a really eye-catching way.

Physically, the texture of foliage in a small kitchen garden is

This porch rail planter is beautiful and interesting, largely by the mix of foliage and fragrance. It contains orange-scented geranium in the center, flanked by the grass-like foliage of chives, and surrounded with interesting foliage textures of oregano, woodruff, and others. Photo courtesy of Pamela Crawford; first appeared in *Easy Container Combos: Herbs & Flowers*

10 Edible Plants with Interesting Textures

Lavender

Basil

Sage

Swiss Chard

Lemon Grass

Fennel

Chives

Rosemary

Dill

Chamomile

10 Fragrant Edible Plants

Lavender

Rosemary

Mint

Roses

Lemon Balm

Thyme

Sage

Apricot

Lemon Verbena

Violets

"The man who has planted a garden feels that he has done something for the good of the world." —Vita Sackville-West

something to think about too. I adore being able to touch my plants. I rub a minty leaf as I walk out to check the mail in the morning or roll a stem of fresh lavender around in my hands after a long afternoon. Many herbs and edibles have amazing textures to consider, and you can put those plants center stage and close at hand.

FRAGRANCE

Another aspect of landscape that I recommend considering is fragrance. I mean, really—is there anything better than a flower that smells like a flower? So many edible herbs and other plants have a pleasing fragrance that it is easy to include plenty of them in your landscape. Choose to place the edible plants with "extra-sensory delights" in areas that are easy to reach. Your garden areas will become wonderlands.

To me, a garden has to be fragrant. There's just something wrong about flowers that don't smell likes themselves. But sometimes more modern hybrids are bred for showy color at the expense of fragrance. This happened, for example, with roses, which usually have the strongest fragrance in the old-fashioned and heirloom varieties. And remember, fragrance can be in the flower or in the foliage. See more in Part III for details about which plants are fragrant or aromatic.

TAKE IT FROM THE TOP—MULTIPLE DIMENSIONS

Another concept that professional landscape designers keep in mind is to consider multiple dimensions. By this I mean not only hard and soft, but also thinking in three dimensions, allowing a line of sight that shows as many of the plants as possible. I love to see vertical gardening elements incorporated into a garden's design. This not only draws the eye all the way to the back of a planter, but also gives you the chance to add more plants in a small space. A win-win!

VERTICAL GROWTH AND PLANT HEIGHT

The general landscaping rule is to place the taller plants toward the back of the planter bed or border, while placing the shorter plants toward the front. Vertical gardening is a way to lift plants higher and create that same effect in a small space. Many people think of edible plants as short, but you can create an entire bed or border with edible plants that have multiple levels. First think about taller shrubs or small trees; They can go in the middle or back of a planter bed or border. For example mulberry, elderberry, camellia, sunflowers, and large shrub roses all can fall within the 8–20 feet range.

For mid-level shrubs or large perennials, you could consider larger edibles and herbs. Think about taller rosemary (there

Even a cutting garden with flowers of similar height can have increased interest by adding vertical obelisks and fruit trees to draw the eye. Photo of the Rotary Garden, courtesy of All-America Selections.

are dwarf varieties too), sage plants, echinacea, artichoke, and tomatoes. Any of these can mix into a cottage garden easily without seeming out of place.

When you look for shorter plants around the edges of the bed or border, think about smaller plants and herbs that won't be covered when they are up near the front. Some of my favorites to consider would be Alpine strawberries, chives, thyme, and calendula.

Don't forget about sneaking vines into the garden too! The cool thing about climbing plants and vines is that you can add height without taking up a lot of space. I've used climbing roses in narrow borders behind the typical row of evergreen boxwoods to create more interest. I've also seen thin wire added to a brick wall to allow honeysuckle or sweet

pea vines to climb up a sunny spot. Consider cucumbers or small melons on a larger fence.

Another way to incorporate vertical gardening could be as simple as adding hanging plants and porch rail containers with small edibles. By using a variety of plants with differing sizes you create multiple levels to draw your eye. In later Chapter 5, I discuss many individual vines and ground covers you can include in an edible landscape. Be sure to check the potential maximum size of the plants you want to grow! Once you begin to take these into consideration it's easy to make note as you select your plants.

Do you always put the tallest in back and the shortest in front? Not always! Thin and wispy foliage, for example, could go nearer to the front if you have bold, attractive foliage behind

Even a border that is primarily vegetables can be arranged in this fashion. Here tomatoes make up the backdrop, while mid-levels are filled with a variety of attractive edibles. Ground covers include greens and squash vines. Photo courtesy of Alfred Diem.

that add beauty and interest. Let's look at some common elements and how to use them around your home.

Paths, Borders, and Edges

These finishing touches add a lot to the beauty of the garden. Whether it's a simple crushed gravel walkway or a more elaborate stone pathway that will last longer and be a more permanent part of the garden. Some common organic and natural materials for simple garden pathways include mulch, straw, or wood chips. These items will have to be replenished or freshened from time to time and are more likely to suffer from bad weather or muddy conditions. Common inorganic materials are bricks, stones, paver rocks, or gravel and the benefits of using these in your garden is that they will last longer.

10 Edibles that Make Good Hanging Basket Plants

Cucumbers

Eggplants

Tomatoes

Small Squash

Zucchini

Begonia

Thyme

Sweet Potatoes

Parsley

Nasturtium

it. You can also have planters with nooks and crannies to create movement; straight lines drive the eye forward quickly but curving, varied heights can hold the gaze and create more interest.

INCORPORATING HARDSCAPING

Hardscaping is a great way to add structure and dimension to the garden landscape. These include not only fences and porch rails, but also arbors, vertical structures, and raised beds. Even permanent edging borders around a garden bed could be considered part of the hardscape elements

Vertical Elements for Climbers

I love to add height to the garden. Many of my favorite designs include weaving in vertical pieces. This can be as simple as a homemade teepee as a temporary climbing structure for an annual vine like cucumbers or squash, or as elaborate as a sturdy arbor to support a grape vine used as a permanent shade plant in your back patio area.

It is important to match the weight and sturdiness of the arbor or trellis with the weight of the plant that it will be supporting because some climbers can be very heavy. It is also important to consider whether

This simple pathway nicely complements the single-plant hedge of roses in the Carver Garden. Photo courtesy of Missouri Botanical Garden.

the climbing vine you want to support is an annual, perennial, or a large shrub like a climbing rose. That way, temporary climbing structures are paired with plants that are temporary actors on your garden's stage.

Raised Beds and Planters

Often the siding or building material you choose for any raised beds or planters can help complement the style of your home and garden. Bricks, set in a formal arrangement, are perfect for traditional, formal designs. Natural stone or rough-hewn wood has a more organic and informal feeling. I've also seen plastic sheets or even sheet metal used as the sides of raised bed planters and each brings its own unique feeling to the area.

Many roof gardens rely solely on raised bed planters for gardening space. Also if you are dealing with an area of your yard that has very poor soil, a raised bed can be a quick shortcut to getting plantable soil almost immediately. I also recommend raised beds for plants that require excellent drainage or in areas where your soil is too damp for more edibles. If you want to save on costs, you can use whatever materials you have on hand or are able to scrounge up. Otherwise you might want to purchase materials specifically designed to complement the aesthetic you wish to achieve.

Fences and Walls

I couldn't talk about hardscaping without mentioning some of the most permanent features you have to deal with in the landscape. When you're landscaping around your home, the walls of your home are fixed and can't be easily (read that "inexpensively") changed or altered in makeup. A brick home is a brick home and depending on the style of your home, you could choose to plant a garden to match.

Later you'll see a picture of our new home's front area—pretty

This simple garden teepee is made from sturdy cedar stakes that are naturally water resistant. It goes up in under an hour and can be easily taken down after fall frosts kill the vine and is stored or moved to another location in the garden.

This edible landscape is greatly complemented by a sturdy, old-fashioned picket fence. Photo courtesy of M. Williams, founder of A Moveable Garden.

red door, brick walls, and wood trim. It's plain right now with landscaping that feeds neither belly nor soul, so this front area will be one of the first places I tackle. See the illustration on page 36 for an example of how I could landscape this area with an edible landscape design.

Fences play a huge part in a landscape design as well. They define specific areas, draw the eye with leading lines, and provide a backdrop for plants. Sometimes they provide a climbing structure for plants as well or help support taller perennials that might otherwise break or fall over in strong winds. Fences alter the climate in the garden by creating microclimates (see Chapter 3) and help you further demonstrate your unique sense of style.

Whenever you plan a new garden area or revamp an existing landscape design, consider how your hardscaping features will complement your style. They also provide interest year round so make them attractive! In winter they will show up more as central elements, while in summer they will become the background for the show stopping flowers and foliage.

COLOR CONSIDERATIONS

Color is definitely something I like to keep in mind in the garden. Many of the original kitchen gardens were rather eclectic in nature, with a helter-skelter modge-podge of whatever plants were handy. However, I like to bring a little bit more refinement to a design by paying attention to when a plant blooms and what color it is when it blooms. We are fortunate to be gardening in the modern era with access to many more cultivars from around the world with a variety of colors.

This basic color wheel shows the primary and secondary colors. There are several ways to break up this basic color wheel for your potential garden color schemes. Let's look at several of these examples in action.

Warm and Cool Color Schemes

The color wheel can be essentially divided in half and grouped into "warm colors" and

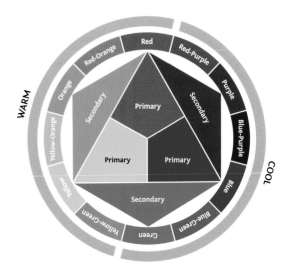

Basic Color Wheel—Note the layout of the warm and cool colors along the wheel.

These Cheyenne Spirit Echinacea show how warm colors create excitement and brighten up a garden space. Photo courtesy of All-America Selections.

breathing space for the eye. Cool colors tend to recede as well and create the illusion of more distance, a trick you can use to make a smaller garden area appear larger.

In fact, some color theories refer to warm colors as "active" and cool colors as "passive," which should help you visualize ways to use them. Both warm and cool colors have a place in a well-planned garden design. Neutral colors that balance warm and cool colors would include gray, brown, and most greens. Other color scheme considerations focus on how the colors interact with each other.

Harmonious or Analogous Color Schemes

As anyone who's graduated from kindergarten will remember, primary colors are the foundation of all the colors on the color wheel—red, blue, and yellow. Then the secondary colors are those halfway between: orange (between red and yellow), green (between yellow and blue), and purple (between blue and red). Knowing this sets the stage for the next color scheme, and one of my favorites.

Analogous colors are the colors that fall between two primary colors. This is sometimes also called a harmonious color scheme, which I to-

"cool colors." This can be one easy way to loosely group your plants into simple but well-defined color schemes of cool and warm colors. By having one garden bed with only warm colors or cool colors, you'll easily tell whether a specific plant is a good fit for the garden, while keeping it simple for you to add plants whenever you find something fun you want to try.

Warm colors are the reds, yellows, and oranges. This would also include things like chartreuse green foliage or orangey terra-cotta containers. Warm colors tend to excite and catch the eye. They make excellent accent colors.

Cool colors include purple, blue, and pink. These tend to soothe and relax and create a

"Look deep into nature, and then you will understand everything better."

—Albert Einstein

Cool colors create a calming, expansive feel in the landscape design. Here purples and grays combine via sage, lavender, and creeping thyme. Photo courtesy of Alexis Watters, founder of BeanandBee.com.

tally adore and sounds way more gardeny than "analogous." An example of a harmonious color scheme in a garden might be plants with blooms and colors from red to blue. That would incorporate red, red-purple, purple, deep violet, and blue colors.

Harmonious color schemes work no matter which

This beautiful landscape features Charlotte, a David Austin rose in a fabulously designed garden area. Photo courtesy of David Austin Roses.

This grouping of echinacea and catmint is a great example of harmonious color schemes. Since the colors are near each other on the color wheel they look good together. Photo courtesy of M. Williams, founder of A Moveable Garden.

slice of the color wheel pie you use. Red, orange, and yellow go together well, as do yellow, green, and blue. Whichever colors you enjoy the most, you can combine them by taking any third of the color. This leaves a lot of room for you to add new plants into the mix. And it is not much more limited than the above warms or cools.

Other Ways to Break Up the Color Wheel

There are a lot of other ways to slice the color wheel and all these options are a little more limiting than the first two we looked at but can create beautiful color schemes for your bed or border.

A complementary color scheme takes colors from across the color wheel. For example blue and orange, or yellow and purple. These complementary colors have a strong contrast and tend to be very eye-catching.

Triadic color schemes take three colors, equally spaced around the color wheel. One of my favorites is violet, red-orange, and yellow-green. For example, chartreuse foliage combines beautifully with red-orange flowers or deep-purple flowers and many landscape designers will even blend that bright green foliage with burgundy foliage for longer-lasting contrast. When you see this, it's a triadic color scheme at work!

What about white and gray? Gray and brown fall into the neutral category

This beautiful summer vignette consists of Gold Standard hosta, Petite Delight monarda, and Hab Gray sedum. Sedums are ornamental but well-suited for mixing into a blended landscape and drought tolerant. The contrast of the lime hosta foliage and burgundy sedum are a stunning backdrop for the edible bee balm. Photo courtesy of M. Williams, founder of A Moveable Garden.

and will basically blend with everything. Gray is often considered a cool color but it can mix well with any color scheme and provides a resting place for the eye. White is neither warm nor cool and it will blend with any color scheme as well. White tends to lighten and brighten so if you have darker foliage, lots of strong or deep colors, adding white to the area can help balance everything nicely.

Ultimately, whether you follow a specific color theme for each garden area or a more eclectic, cottage-garden style is completely up to you. But understanding how color plays a part in the way your garden looks will help you make the best design decisions for your unique situation.

Playing with landscape design is a lifelong addiction for gardeners. You may never feel completely finished with a space and each year you'll make tweaks and additions. You may find gaps in a season where there's not as much interest as you'd like or you want to change things up. That's totally normal. The most important thing is to take the first steps and get started with your garden areas!

3

Gardening Basics — How Do I Plant a Garden Anyway?

"Okay, Angela," you might be saying, "this sounds awesome and I'm ready to get planting, but I do not have a green thumb." That's no problem. I'm a recovering brown-thumb myself. But "edible landscaping" does mean gardening, so let's look at the basics.

There are some things that are universal to gardening no matter what you're growing or for what purpose. Once you get these essential foundations figured out, you'll be unstoppable. Sun, soil, water, and growing climates. Wax on, wax off, Young Grasshopper.

ZONES AND CLIMATES AND SUNSHINY DAYS

Gardeners learn very quickly that one of the biggest limitations for their garden is the zone, or gardening climate area in which they live. This basic starting point, along with microclimates and the amount of sun your garden gets, are the things that will create the special limitations of your personal garden.

PLANT COLD HARDINESS ZONES

Gardening zones are loosely delineated areas of the country that are typically based around first and last frost dates, as well as average low temperatures. These hardiness zones tell you the lowest hardiness rating your plants will be able to survive in your area.

So what does this mean for you? It means, simply, that if you live in a zone 7, you will experience weather that is too cold for most zone 8 plants to survive year after year.

Now I live in a zone 7 area—in fact we are zone 7b (the warmer half of zone 7)—and gardeners in my area are notorious for planting more tropical plants that simply do not survive long-term. We'll baby along those citrus trees or sneak in a shrub we know won't make it ten years, just to enjoy the plants during the milder winters we experience on occasion. It's a near obsession.

My friend Angi is in a warmer climate than I am and she can grow this Meyer's lemon in the ground. When I grow this same tree, I have to do so in a container that can be overwintered indoors. Photo courtesy of Angi Schneider.

These peaches are espaliered along a light-colored stone wall, creating a warmer microclimate for them that will protect them from late frosts. Photo courtesy of Alfred Diem.

However, for the beginning gardener and those who, like me, are looking for more low-maintenance gardening fun, I recommend staying well within your hardiness zone designations. Why? Simple—you will have better success trying to grow plants that are able to survive easily in your area.

If you don't already know your gardening zone, that will be your first order of business. Visit UntrainedHousewife.com/GardenZones for more information about how to discover your gardening zone.

MICROCLIMATES: AKA NINJA GARDENING

Microclimates are the secret ninja moves in gardening. They are ways to grow more food and expand the selection you can plant, and also take advantage of naturally occurring "hot spots" or "cool zones" in your garden.

For example, if you put your peach trees on a north-facing slope, you can delay the budding of your trees by a few weeks. In an area with late frosts, this will protect your fruiting buds from being destroyed by cold weather.

Low-lying areas can collect cool air, making the temperature several degrees cooler than the surrounding areas. Large bodies of water can buffer colder climates, releasing warmth and reflecting sunlight to the plants around it.

Taking advantage of some of these tendencies can expand what you can grow in your garden. If you are in Zone 6b and growing a peach tree with a hardiness of Zone 7, you may be able to get away with it on a northern slope beside a pond or riverbank.

On a smaller scale, a windbreak can shield plants from drying winds. A white fence can reflect indirect light into a shadier area, giving you a little more leeway on plant selection. Or a raised bed will warm up sooner in the spring, giving you a place to start your earliest seeds.

SUN VS. SHADE

The next element that will limit and define your gardening capabilities is the amount of sun your garden receives each day. And it's a big limitation.

There are some plants that cannot be grown in shady areas. No matter

"It was such a pleasure to sink one's hands into the warm earth to feel at one's fingertips the possibilities of the new season."

—Kate Morton

Shade may seem like a hindrance to the edible landscape, but this lovely trio of useful plants—hostas, Solomon seal, and ginger (in the background)—prove that heavily dappled shade can be as lovely as sunny borders. Photo courtesy of M. Williams, founder of A Moveable Garden.

- **Sun Plants**—Areas of the yard that gets six or more hours per day are considered "full sun" areas, even if they are actually in shade during some parts of the days.

- **Part Sun**—This means a plant should receive four to six hours of sun per day but will tolerate more shade than a full sun counterpart.

- **Part Shade**—These plants will tolerate four hours of sun but probably need some shade, likely during the hottest parts of the day.

- **Shade**—These plants should not receive more than three hours of sun per day. Even plants labeled "Full Shade" can tolerate a couple hours of sun unless the label directions specifically state "avoid direct sunlight."

Download the free "Garden Journal Pages" from *BackyardFarmingGuide.com*. Print out as many of the grid papers as needed to sketch out the rough shape of the yard and planter areas you will be working with. Do sun checks throughout one entire day and estimate the hours of sun in the various planting areas.

"The soil is the gift of God to the Living." —Thomas Jefferson

how much you water them. No matter how fabulous your soil, tomatoes, for example, need a certain amount of sunlight each day or they will not grow well and will not produce a good amount of fruit. In order to plan your garden spaces, plot out which areas of your yard get sunlight during which parts of the day.

I recommend making a sketch of your home's layout and plotting the sunny and shady areas during different times of the day. Check the yard at 8:00 a.m., 10:00 a.m., noon, 2:00 p.m., 4:00 p.m., 6:00 p.m. and make a notation of where the shady and sunny spots are. Once you have an understanding of spring, summer, and fall sun patterns in the space that you have to work with, you'll better plan which plants can go in what areas.

WATER AND SOIL

Soil quality impacts your garden a great deal. And it's something we need to assess as gardeners to begin making a plan for how to spend our time and money in the garden.

Is the soil around your home rocky? Mostly clay? Sandy? Saturated with chemicals from a neighboring golf course? Near a beach so salty breezes are an issue? We each face a unique soil combination, so where do we start?

WHAT KIND OF SOIL DO YOU HAVE?

One way to get started is figure out what kind of dirt you have in your yard. There are three main kinds.

High-quality loam soil full of organic matter has a rich dark-brown color, particles of differing sizes and looks healthy. Photo courtesy of M. Williams, founder of A Moveable Garden.

I like to give the soil a simple squeeze test to get a good idea of what its makeup is like. Dig a spadeful of moist-but-not-soaking-wet soil and clench your fist around it. When you open up your hand, clay soil will stay smooshed together like a play dough snake, while sandy soil will break apart easily. Loam soil falls between the two. Our new house has excellent soil quality—

The healthy volunteer plant in compost bin proves how nourishing the soil it. Inexpensively created from extra lumber, there's no reason to not have a compost bin going at all times. Photo courtesy of Anne Heideman.

it's something we checked before making a final purchase decision!

OTHER THINGS TO TEST IN YOUR SOIL

Remember that the squeeze-test above is simplistic and limited in what it will reveal to you. You'll know something about the soil composition of the soil, but nothing about the chemicals that might be there. You will only know your soil's foundation, not the window-dressing.

I highly recommend having your soil tested at your local county extension office. You will be able to learn the soil's pH levels, salinity (buildup of salts), nutritional makeup, and any deficiencies. I also recommend testing for herbicide contamination or lead if you're in an area where those things might be a problem

for you. Chatting with your local county extension office will give you a good idea of what typical problems might be in your local area and that will be the best place for you to start.

Soil is so important. I will tell you that when we were considering two different properties for our recent move, we did some at-home tests of the soil in each property to make sure we weren't inheriting something too troublesome.

Keep looking at your soil. Something that is semi-damp, breaks easily into smaller chunks, and has visible organic matter in it is ideal. Often dark and rich-looking and with bits of decaying leaves or even live earth worms in it—these will be your best signs that you have good-quality soil to start things off, and that's a boon for any gardener.

- *Clay Soil*—Clay soil has very fine particles, which hold water tightly. It's often very sticky when wet and very hard when dried. Clay holds water for a long time after watering, but can also make it less available for the roots of plants to absorb the water.

- *Sandy Soil*—Sandy soil has very large particles, often visible to the naked eye as individual grains. Water passes through sand quickly, leaving less water for the roots of the plants. Drainage is very quick. As a result, sandy soils are often less fertile with fewer nutrients and minerals for the plants.

- *Loam soil*—Loamy soil is often considered the best and has a nice mix of particle sizes. Gardeners also expect to see lots of organic materials (bits of bugs and plants) mixed into the soil because this provides lots of nutrients and minerals for the growing plants to use. Loam soil also helps hold water, but not too much, so plants have both water and air for good growth.

Once you have an understanding of your soil's composition, quality, and pH, you can begin to make adjustments as needed.

AMENDING THE SOIL

Amending the soil simply means adding stuff to the dirt of your garden area. Often this takes the form of purchased additives such as lime, bone meal, wood ash, or other concentrated fertilizers. A better way to amend your soil quality is to take every opportunity to add new organic materials to the soil. This means compost, manures, mulches, and more.

Compost—Compost is well-rotted organic matter. Grass clippings, leaves, straw, scrap vegetables from the kitchen, hair clippings, manure of all kinds, and other biodegradable items can all be added to compost bins or heaps. These compost piles then break down through heat and moisture to create rich, loamy compost to work into the soil of your gardens.

Composting seems intimidating to some, but it's simple if you keep the ratio in mind. The quickest compost bins are made of both green and brown materials.

Green materials are high-nitrogen items like chicken, cow, or horse manure, grass clippings, leafy shrub prunings, kitchen scraps, and so on. Items that are considered brown materials are typically dried items lower in nitrogen such as hay, straw, dried leaves, small twigs or wood chips, and so on. Adding both to the compost bin in a nice mix of about a 30:1 ratio will really get your compost bin cooking!

Mulches—Mulches are organic materials that are placed on top of the ground around plants. Mulch helps preserve moisture, block weeds and moderate the temperature of the soil, and it eventually provides more organic materials as the creepy crawlies (and even microscopic critters) in your garden work all the mulch into the soil. Once the ground begins to warm up in the spring, it's the perfect time to refresh the layer of mulch in your garden areas.

I tend to avoid inorganic materials in my mulches since part of my goal as a gardener is to always be adding to the garden. Rocks, plastic chips, gravel, and other inorganic mulches do not help me accomplish this goal and so are avoided.

WATER, WATER, EVERYWHERE

Even as a brown-thumb gardener, I knew that plants need water to survive. What I

GREEN MATERIALS NITROGEN RATIO
• *Grass clippings (20:1)*
• *Chicken Manure (10:1)*
• *Ruminant Manure (20:1)*
• *Wood Ash (25:1)*
• *Veggie Scraps/Weeds (20:1)*

BROWN MATERIALS NITROGEN RATIO
• *Straw/Hay/Wheat stalks (60–80:1)*
• *Sawdust (500:1)*
• *Shredded paper (200:1)*
• *Cardboard (350:1)*
• *Leaves (60:1)*

These tomatoes are well mulched with a thick layer of straw that will preserve moisture once our Oklahoma summer sets in. Note the twine strung to the top of the fence to allow these indeterminate tomatoes to climb.

soil, but will also have lots of nutrients to draw from as well. And a couple days later, thanks to our nice, thick layer of mulch, the plant will *still* have access to water it needs.

We prefer to use a soaker hose–style irrigation system, which can be fairly inexpensive to set up, for all our major beds, borders, and garden areas. By putting the water directly into the soil around the plant, you greatly reduce any wasted water from evaporation, run-off, and misdirected sprinklers. It might not seem like a lot in one watering session, but it can really add up over the course of the entire year.

didn't understand is how the other factors—soil composition and organic matter—play a huge role in how much water is available for the plants. And, as we'll see a little later on, the way we water can also impact how much water we use.

A cup of water poured into a container full of sand will quickly drain away, taking any nutrients or minerals out of the soil as well, leaving the plant with little usable water after just a few minutes. A cup of water poured into a clay soil will leave the container filled with water for a long time, but all the air compressed from the soil means the plant drowns itself and cannot use the water surrounding it.

But with a loamy soil with plenty of compost mixed into it, this same plant will not only have plenty of access to the water in the

I also do not put my watering on an automated system. Have you ever seen someone's sprinklers going off in the middle of a rainstorm? Don't be that guy. Just don't. When your plants need to be watered, turn on the soaker hose, wait until it's done, and then turn it off. For us, with the water flow system we have, that's about thirty minutes to water the garden. In the spring and fall it's only needed about once a week. In our brutal, dry Oklahoma summers, we might be watering every other day. A quick check during our morning walk around the garden tells us

If your soil isn't the right composition, it will impact the amount of water your plants receive—no matter how much it rains or you water them.

soon enough whether we need to run the water or not.

Container plants that don't have the benefit of deeper roots and protection from drying winds will need to be watered more frequently. In Oklahoma once we hit 100-degree-plus weather I've even had to water my smaller containers twice a day—especially on windy days, which dry plants out much faster.

To check if your plants need to be watered, look at the soil. Scratch a little bit beneath a surface—just a fingertip will do. If there's dampness still in the soil you're good to go. If it feels drier than a completely wrung

out sponge, you may need to go ahead and water. Pretty simple right? Just get in the habit of checking every day.

I tend to check in the mornings with my morning cup of coffee and stroll out to the mailbox. Your best time of the day might be in the afternoon when the kids get home from school. Whatever works for you!

Now that you've learned all the foundations of landscape design and the basics of gardening, it's time to level up. In the next chapter you'll begin to see how all these pieces come together as we explore some potential designs and considerations in all the various areas around your home.

The plants in this entryway door container garden will need more frequent watering than if they were planted directly in the ground. Keeping containers in easy reach makes it a simpler task. Photo courtesy of Liz West.

PART II

*Original Edible
Garden Designs —
Ninja Warrior Plans*

Every gardening ninja needs a plan of attack, and in these next pages you will see some of the original garden designs I've created. Not only have I used my own home as the dimensions for these plans, but I've included you in the entire process from start to finish. You'll learn the thought process that goes into creating a beautiful garden design that is fruitful and bountiful. Look for spotlights of successful gardeners around the nation who are doing amazing things with their gardens for further inspiration.

4

Tour of the House – Ninja Style

Now that you've seen the benefits of edible landscaping, how to plan a dramatic and interesting garden design, and learned the basics of gardening in general, let's have some fun and really tie it all together. Let's look at how someone who just moved into a brand-new house, like myself, might sit down and plan a design that will create gorgeous landscaped areas that are also productive. We're going to take a tour around the entire house. And in doing so, we'll tackle some tricky spots! Growing areas that are difficult won't stop us in the slightest.

This long, sturdy ranch-style house just needs some redesigning of the front landscape to be much more graceful and appealing to the eye.

As the photo above shows, the house is long and boxy with an odd grassy area between the driveway and front porch. By remaking the front planter (shown here with shrubs removed) to coordinate with the transitional space and adding some curves, the entire curb appeal is enhanced.

First Impressions First—Foundation Planter

PART SUN/PART SHADE

Of course, the first impression of a home is so important. Traditional landscaping often centers around creating simple foundation plantings. These Stepford-wife style plantings are usually boring, uninspiring, and filled with repetition in all the wrong ways. If you've taken it up a notch, you have gorgeous landscape designs but probably have very few, if any, edibles incorporated into the plantings.

This original design will show you how I plan to transform a currently boring foundation hedge into a sweeping, highly ornamental planting. I'll be facing some challenges. For example, my new house is a long, ranch-style home that can end up looking boxy if not dressed properly. This boxy effect is currently not helped at all by the existing overgrown hedge bushes. That's the first thing that has to be fixed!

The other major challenge is that the eastward facing front of the house is part sun to part shade. This means the area of the

planters nearest the house lose light around noon or 1:00 p.m. at the latest in the summer months. The areas further from the house will lose light between 1:00–3:30 p.m. depending on the time of the year and how far from the home you are. Plenty of light for lush lawn means I have a wide variety of edibles that will tolerate the part sun.

As the view from the street shows in the photograph above, there is only a very small planting area. A 4-foot-wide strip hugs the foundation of the house where the shrubs once hung over the 2-foot-wide sidewalk to nowhere. In front of the house, there is also an odd triangle section between the driveway and entryway porch, on the right side of the front door (see photo on page 36). The challenge for me was creating each unique space in a way that would look coordinated together, but still be it's own space.

If you look at the design (see page 36), you'll see that the first thing I'll do is remove the completely unnecessary concrete sidewalk. Then the front of the house will have a little more breathing room and better drainage when it rains, and I'll be able to create a more sweeping line for the planting.

PLANTING THE TRANSITIONAL SPACE

This first area is the very transitional space between the driveway and the patio and the entry and the house and the lawn. There are some considerations I kept in mind when designing this space. It needs to look good from every angle. It needs to not block my view of the front yard from the living room window. And it needs to include some nice fragrant and visually appealing plants.

The Transitional Space

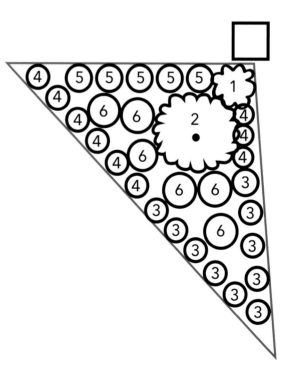

1. Scarlet Running Beans
2. Hibiscus – dwarf variety like 'Summer Storm' or Summerific® Cherry Cheesecake
3. Thyme – Archer's Gold or Lemon Thyme
4. Chives – Fine Leaf Chives
5. New Zealand Spinach
6. Daylily – All-American Baby
7. Container planted with Sicilian Sunshine™ Sweet Bay

1. Scarlet Runner Beans
(*Phaseolus Coccineus*)—
Annual Vine

Like all vining beans, these annuals are frost sensitive and will need to be replanted every year. My design doesn't rely on them; however, during the spring and summer, these climbers will add vertical interest and take advantage of the porch leg. They are light climbers that won't overwhelm a single support beam. And scarlet runners are absolutely gorgeous—bright red blooms stand out against a fresh green color climbing up in a tangled delight on whatever trellis is provided.

2. Hibiscus (*Hibiscus* hybrid)—
Perennial Shrub

Some cultivars of hibiscus will tolerate more shade than others and by skewing this plant slightly forward in the planter it will get five-plus hours of sun each day in my zone 7 garden. Choose a shrub hardy for your area and a color that you like. I'm choosing a blush pink blooming cultivar with darker center that will stand

These lovely hibiscus are *Hibiscus syriacus* Helene. Photo by Lisa Francis, courtesy of Missouri Botanical Garden.

out against the red brick of my home. Summerific® Cherry Cheesecake is a Proven Winner variety hardy in zones 4–9 and Lil' Kim™ Rose of Sharon by Monrovia is hardy in zones 5–8 and has similarly colored blooms of smaller size but the reddish-pink eye is concentrated only in the center of the bloom. Both will stay in the 3–5 foot range.

3. Thyme (*Thymus*)—
Perennial Herb

One of my favorite ground covers of all time, I've chosen creeping thyme as a ground cover and edging on the sunniest side of this planter. It will naturally be limited according to the amount of sunlight, but will provide evergreen interest throughout the year. There are several varieties you could choose for this space, but I will stick with something 2–6 inches tall. For this space I'll choose one of the lime-green foliage varieties for the color contrast; Lemon Frost (zones 5–11), which has white summer flowers; *Thymus citriodorus* Lime (Zones 5–9), which has a citrusy fragrance and pink blooms; or *Thymus pulegioides* Archer's Gold (Zones 5–9), which has purple-blue flowers and grows taller up to 6 inches. See Chapter 5 for more thyme suggestions.

Scarlet runner beans create a gorgeous backdrop for the other plants and the red blooms pick up the red from the container. This photo first appeared in *Easy Container Combos: Vegetables & Flowers* and is used courtesy of Pamela Crawford.

"One of the healthiest ways to gamble is with a spade and a package of seeds."

—Dan Bennett

This is without a doubt one of my favorite garden ground covers. Here Lime thyme contrasts beautifully with chives. Photo courtesy of Baker Creek Seeds.

4. Chives
(*Allium schoenoprosum*)—
Perennial Herb

This pretty little perennial herb is also evergreen in some areas and will be hardy in zones 3–9, making it quite winter hardy. The strappy, bright foliage is similar to green onions but typically much smaller. The flowers are beautiful purple, white, or pink globe-shaped flower clusters. You could try Fine Leaf Chives, which are only about 1–2 inches tall with classic purple-pink flower; Silver Chimes with nearly white flowers and more diminutive size; or even Forescate, which has a brighter pink color and full size leaves.

5. New Zealand Spinach
(*Tetregonia expansa*)—
Herbaceous Perennial

New Zealand spinach is not related to spinach, but it does taste similar to spinach and can be used like spinach in cooked recipes. New Zealand spinach is considered an herbaceous perennial. In mild climates it will be evergreen, producing edible greens year round. Harvest the top shoots for eating and leaving the woodier outside leaves to produce energy for the plant. New Zealand spinach will grow 1–2 feet tall and wide, and will form a pleasant ground cover mat. Some varieties have more of a trailing growth habit, which makes it lovely as an edging for containers or raised beds. It grows well in part shade, although growth rate will be slower in shadier spots—which is ideal for me since I can continue harvesting it as needed throughout the majority of the growing season.

Chives blooms are typically a pretty lavender-purple like these, but are also available in pink and white forms. Photo by Liz West.

6. Daylily (*Hemerocalis*)—
Flowering Perennial

Daylilies are a hardy, perennial plant with interesting, grass-like foliage and beautiful blooms. They get their name because of their blooming habit—each flower will bloom for just one day. Don't let that fool you though! Daylily plants can bloom for weeks on end because each individual plant will produce many flowers throughout the growing season.

Daylilies are sometimes evergreen and sometimes deciduous; it often depends on the growing zone you're in. For our purposes I will choose evergreen varieties that will hold their color longer during the winter months. There are thousands of varieties to choose from, so you'll easily find a color you love in a daylily best suited to your region.

These peach-colored All-American Baby daylilies would go well with the rest of my design, but there are many colors and sizes to choose from. Photo by Ashley DeRousse courtesy of Missouri Botanical Garden.

All sweet bay shrubs have attractive foliage but this golden leaved cultivar will pop against my red brick home. Photo courtesy of Proven Winners.

7. Bay Laurel (*Laurus nobilis*)—
Woody Shrub

Sweet bay is a useful culinary herb but not hardy in my zones as it grows best in zones 8–10. However, the variety Sicilian Sunshine™ by Proven Winners makes a great container planter so I can overwinter it in the garage or even on the enclosed back porch. The benefits of a named cultivar like this one are that they can be a little smaller for container growing. This has unique bright gold foliage that will complement the lime-green thyme ground cover I chose and pop against the red bright wall.

"Plants want to grow; they are on your side as long as you are reasonably sensible."

—Anne Wareham

"The greatest gift of the garden is the restoration of the five senses."

—Hanna Rion

Transitional and Odd Spaces
This transitional space is small but it will pack a punch of color and interest when properly managed.

FRONT YARD FOUNDATION PLANTING REMADE

Bringing life into the new foundation planter is actually fun. I just love transforming boring rows of hedges into something more interesting. Here are some of the plants I could include in this garden design. Remember to check Part 3 for some of my favorite edible landscape plants to make your own choices. I'll share my thought process in why I chose what I chose, and you can use similar reasoning to make substitutions if needed.

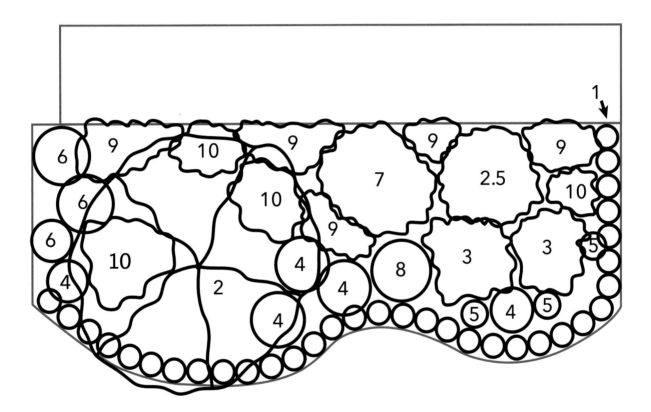

1. Alpine Strawberries
2. Cornelian Cherry Dogwood
2.5 *Camellia sinensis*
3. Evergreen Blueberries – Legacy and Bountiful Blue®
4. Daylily – All-American Baby
5. Sorrel "Profusion"
6. Rosemary
7. Elderberry – Black Lace™
8. Container planted with Basil and Mint
9. Sweet Woodruff
10. Wild Ginger

1. Alpine Strawberries
(*Fragaria vesca*)—
Herbaceous Perennials

These are some of my favorite edging plants and they are hardy in zones 4–10 (some to zone 11). These diminutive strawberries tend to be clumping, rather than spreading by runners, making them easy to manage in the garden landscape. The foliage stays beautiful year-round, and small white flowers are followed by delicious, tiny fruit June through first frost.

2. Cornelian Cherry Dogwood
(*Cornus mas*)—
Fruit Tree/Shrub

Hardy zones 3–8, this dogwood relation has small, edible fruits that make excellent sauces and jellies. I once enjoyed this as a sauce drizzled over pancakes at a friend's house and have wanted to plant one ever since. This foundation remodel is my chance because the Cornelian cherry dogwood easily tolerates part shade. Pruning will keep the slow-growing tree easily to a 12–15 foot tall and wide, or a naturally dwarfed form like Nana can be planted. With gorgeous yellow flowers on naked branches, this dogwood will take the place of forsythia in the landscape, and the bright red berries that follow are delicious, not-too-sweet edibles.

Strawberries make great edging plants because their flowers are quite attractive, and they're followed by delicious fruit. Photo courtesy of M. Williams, founder of A Moveable Garden.

During winter the red-tinged scaly bark adds plenty of interest.

If you are in a more southern zone, the tree won't set fruit or flowers because it requires some chill hours. For zones 8b and higher, choose a different tree for the accent piece in this design such as a dwarf lemon or pineapple guava.

2.5 Tea Camellia (*Camellia sinensis*)—
Evergreen Shrub

Camellia sinensis is a camellia shrub with less-ornamental flowers, though the shrub itself is beautiful with lovely evergreen foliage. It has been used for hundreds of years for tea. Black tea, green tea, and so on is made from harvesting the tips of the growing branches. This will provide a good foundational color near the home's entrance.

While this particular Cornelian Cherry is growing in the woods, you can see how it will make an excellent accent tree in front of the red brick house. Gorgeous yellow flowers in later winter are stunning. Photo courtesy of Alfred Diem.

3. Evergreen Blueberry
(*Vaccinium* varied)—
Fruit Shrub

Blueberries are a hidden gem in the landscaping community. Named cultivars provide a huge variation with zone hardiness from 3–10 depending on the variety and cultivar you choose. For this particular design, I've chosen a larger cultivar Legacy, which reaches 6 feet for the back and a smaller variety such as Bountiful Blue® for the front, which tops out at 3 feet maximum. This will give depth and dimension because of the varied heights, as well as assisting in cross-pollination, resulting in more fruit for each bush.

See the section on blueberries for more information about their use in the landscape. If the part sun area here ends up being too much shade for good fruiting, I could replace them with an evergreen huckleberry (*Vaccinium ovatum*), which, in addition to better fruiting in shady conditions, also has beautiful foliage popular as greenery in cut flower arrangements.

4. Daylily (*Hemerocalis*)—
Flowering Perennial

Daylilies are rock stars in the edible garden landscape. If I use the same cultivar as the one I chose above, these daylilies will help tie the two spaces on either side of the door together to create a cohesive appearance.

5. Sorrel (*Rumex acetosa*)—
Perennial Herb

Sorrel is a perennial herb that is hardy to zone 3 and even further with some winter protection. There are a few different varieties that have been used for centuries for their tangy, lemon-flavored leaves in stews, salads, and pestos, but my favorite is a named cultivar called Profusion. Profusion is a sterile variety that doesn't set seeds so the leaves don't turn bitter during the summer. Without the summer flower spikes, it also forms a tidier, clump form that looks neater in a foundation planting.

6. Rosemary
(*Romarinus officinalis*)—
Woody Perennial Herb

Rosemary, one of my favorite landscape plants of all time, is a hardy, evergreen, and perennial herb that has the potential to grow quite large in the landscape. Hardy in zones 4–10, my cooler zone 7 garden keeps our rosemary to a smaller 3–4 feet tall and wide. However, I've seen them almost twice as wide in a zone 10 garden. Here I've placed rosemary on the sunny side of this border, where it should thrive and provide a nice counterpoint to the shadier evergreens near the front door. I think the Golden or Golden Rain rosemary would go nicely here because it has bright yellow-green leaves that would echo the other lime-colored foliage I've included in this design.

Blueberries are one of my favorite shrubs for sunny or light shade areas. They are gorgeous and delicious at the same time.

One of my favorites—this is a gorgeous herb with interesting, fragrant, and evergreen foliage. Photo courtesy of Missouri Botanical Garden.

7. Elderberry (*Sambucus nigra*)— Fruiting Shrub

One of my favorite understory or woodland shrubs, the elderberry grows wild in my area. In fact we often see it blooming in the fencerows along highways and near creek banks in the spring, and we've used both flowers and berries. The cultivar I've chosen for this landscape design isn't one you'd see growing natively, however! The Black Lace™ by Proven Winners has not only all the benefits of the wild elderberry, but also unique colors that stand out in the garden. But most of all, I love this elderberry for the dark burgundy, almost black, fine-cut foliage that makes a gorgeous backdrop for the bright pink flower clusters.

New elderberry cultivars are available with beautifully colored foliage like this Black Lace™ by Proven Winners. Check each cultivar for suitability as an edible before adding to your edible landscape. Photo courtesy of Proven Winners.

8. Basil and Mint— Container Planter

To draw the eye to the landscape designs on both sides of the door, I'll be using a similarly colored planter as the one I planted my sweet bay in. Mint makes an excellent container plant because it spreads so invasively without some boundaries. And basil is so lovely with so many uses in the kitchen, I always love to keep some growing right outside the door. This container will do that beautifully. I will

Even simple basil leaves are a beautiful green that's perfect for container plantings.

use two basil varieties in my oversized container: Dwarf Greek, which has a naturally rounded size and small leaves to contrast with Corsican, a purple and green broader leaf variety. True spearmint (*Minta spectica*) rounds out this container with a variety of contrasting foliage types and colors.

9. Sweet Woodruff (*Galium odoratum*)— Ground Cover

Sweet woodruff is hardy in zones 4–8 and in the warmest zones it will stay evergreen. It's naturally a woodland ground cover so it works well under the other perennials and shrubs in this foundation planting. The bright, sweetly fragrant white flowers look beautiful over the fresh green foliage. It dries well for sachets and potpourri, and the flowers are historically used to flavor spring wines.

10. Wild Ginger (*Asarum caudatum*)— Evergreen Ground Cover

Slower-growing than the sweet woodruff above, wild ginger will still spread and naturalize. I love the cheerful, heart-shaped leaves and the evergreen color they provide in the garden. I will plant more of this ginger than the sweet woodruff, to make sure it doesn't get crowded out. It's a gorgeous ground cover with pretty, glossy leaves.

Overall, this garden design adds repeating pops of color with the bright yellow-green foliage, has some beautiful evergreens, blooms through most of the season, and has fragrant, interesting plants near the door where they can be enjoyed on a regular basis. Harvesting some tea or collecting fresh herbs is as simple as stepping out my front door where they can be fingertip handy. The curves of the bed shape, paired with the pretty, interesting plant forms, will soften the long, somewhat harsh lines of my ranch-style home.

Glossy, evergreen ground cover for shady spots. Photo courtesy of Liz West.

Beautiful Foundation Border

This enlarged front planter now has space for beautiful edible trees and shrubs and will tie with the transitional space with matching daylilies and containers.

Low Maintenance Mailbox Planter
(DROUGHT-TOLERANT, FRAGRANT, FULL-SUN)

Mailboxes can be incredibly boring or beautiful with lovely plantings. The worst possible thing is the lovely plants that die and wither away after a couple weeks and look miserable. Whoops! Ninja gardeners plant the right things in the right spaces so that they are well suited for the area and don't drive you crazy trying to take care of them.

This simple design brings together drought-tolerant plants that prefer well-draining soil and tolerate going days or even weeks without supplemental watering and still look amazing. Plants are also chosen for their long bloom times so you will have weeks of colors. I will use interesting landscaping rocks to build the raised planter so there's interest from the hardscaping as well as the plants.

1. Echinacea—Perennial Herb

I love echinacea flowers. They are slower to appear in the spring so I'd probably

CAUTION: Just as with the parking strip design, I would caution against using edible plants grown in areas with high-traffic from cars for internal use. Where there's high probability of pollution from wandering dogs or lots of vehicles, you probably want to avoid using them for food. I will use these blooms as cut-flowers—pretty!

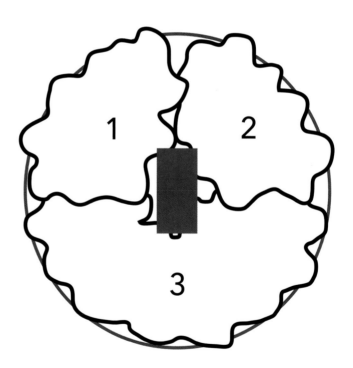

1. Lavender – FERNLEAF LAVENDER   2. Echinacea – STARLIGHT
3. Thyme – WOOLLY THYME

A simple raised bed around the mailbox can provide a low-maintenance, fragrant garden full of blooms.

underplant these herbs with violas that will self-seed and have good fall-spring color in our hot-summer areas. Meanwhile, for all of summer and well into fall, an echinacea will produce large, daisy-like flowers with a variety of cultivars available to choose from. My design will use Starlight, which looks great in cut-flower bouquets since I won't be using this space to grow internally-consumed edibles

2. Lavender
(*Lavandula spp.*)— Perennial Herb

Lavender is a Mediterranean plant so it's suited to well-draining soil. If you're in an area with higher-than-average rainfall, you would need to plant them in a raised bed or replace with something else that can tolerate wet-feet better. I've found that this herb easily tolerates the hot summers in my area, so it's a go-to for me. I plan to use *Lavandula multifida*, which is a fernleaf lavender that has more fine-cut foliage and great contrast with the Echinacea. I also love the contrast in the shape of the flowers. They will both bloom for many weeks throughout the summer and fall.

3. Thyme
(*Thymus* spp.)— Perennial Evergreen Ground Cover

As you've already noticed, I love thyme in the garden. It's a great full-sun, low-maintenance ground cover that is perfect for the front edge of this raised mailbox planter. The evergreen color will keep interest year-round, and the fragrance will make it a nice treat every time you go to the mailbox. Archer's Gold is really pretty and holds its color well, and Woolly Thyme usually has profuse flowering that coordinates with this design beautifully and drape nicely over the edges of the planter.

Echinacea, like the other plants in this simple design, will attract pollinators to the garden and support beneficial insects. Photo courtesy of M. Williams, Founder of A Moveable Garden.

Lavender is one of my favorite summer-blooming, fragrant perennials, and it blends well with many other plants in the landscape. Photo by Amanda Beal courtesy of Missouri Botanical Garden.

Low-Maintenance and Drought-Tolerant Planter

Any planter or container that is away from the house will need lower-maintenance plants in them.

BEFORE —Before the edible landscape design, this space was the sunniest area of Sue's yard, but not being put to good use. Photo courtesy of Sue St Jean, founder of www.LessNoise-MoreGreen.com

Sue St. Jean
Rhode Island, Zone 6B

Edible Front Yard Garden

Located in an urban setting, in a neighborhood consisting of Victorian homes, this edible landscape was born out of the desire to grow food in the sunniest part of the property: the front yard. The property's shady traditional vegetable beds, located in the backyard, were at growing capacity, while the south facing front yard, consisting of lawn, yews, and hosta was bathed in sun. In 2014, the entire front yard was removed and seven cubic square yards of compost was added to the soil. The resulting garden consists of two spaces either side of a pathway leading to the porch. To keep with the tone of the neighborhood, a formal garden design was created, with the same plants installed on each side in a mirror image of each other. Two diamond-shaped brick walkways were added to allow access to all areas and to provide visual interest in the winter.

AFTER — Sue's new garden is in keeping with the formal feel of the neighborhood but has many delightful edibles hidden in the design. Photo courtesy of Sue St Jean, founder of www.LessNoise-MoreGreen.com.

The gardens contain over sixty varieties of plants, 85 percent of which are a mix of herbs, berries, vegetables, and edible flowers. Juniper spruces and rhododendrons line the foundation to add evergreen color in the winter while the middle of each diamond walkway is filled with annual vegetables. Mostly fruiting vegetables are included: eggplant, peppers, and squash to minimize holes in the design when harvesting, as well as kales and Swiss chards. Three varieties of strawberries, lingonberries, thyme, and oregano make perfect ground cover plants, which were essential additions to help solve soil erosion issues caused by the turning in of all the yards of compost! Favorites in the garden include Black Lace Elderberry, which has stunning purple foliage and pink flowers, edible Bachelor's Buttons, Peppermint Swiss chard with brilliant pink stems, and perennial Victoria rhubarb—the perfect foundation plant. The resulting edible landscape creates both a beautiful and productive welcome to the home and has sparked much interest and positive comments from neighbors, who are surprised to learn that the "beautiful garden" is, in fact, food production in disguise.

PATIO OR DECK DESIGN
(FULL-SUN, ANNUALS + PERENNIALS, CONTAINERS, AND RAISED BEDS)

This design, like the mailbox planter, relies on raised beds and a container garden design. While it assumes a full-sun location, it also assumes more frequent maintenance and care than the mailbox planter. It will be nearer the back door and in an area where we would be hanging out as a family or entertaining guests. The annuals and vegetables will need to be rotated out often because the plants die or look weedy. We will be most actively using this area spring-fall, so there's less concern with winter interest.

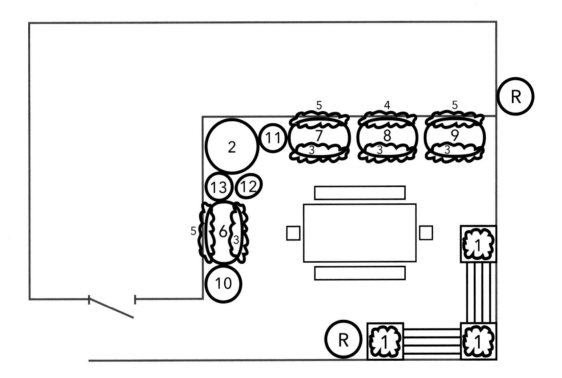

1. Grapes on arbors built over benches
2. Meyer's Lemon in large container
3. Nasturtium and Creeping Oregano or Marjoram
4. Peas and Beans up the trellis
5. Squash up the trellis
6. Parsley and Arugula
7. Swiss Chard
8. Dwarf Tomatoes
9. Sage, Dill, and Lemon Grass
10. Aloe Vera and Calendula
11. Fish Peppers
12. Giant Red Japanese Mustard
13. Ping Tung Eggplant

This design relies on raised beds and planters to create the outdoor garden area, which can be built on any patio or deck area. We'll underlay ours with flagstone but you can adapt this to a wooden deck, brick, or concrete.

1. Grapes
(*Vitus* spp.)— Perennial Vining Fruit

The grapes are planted on arbors that go over the benches. These sturdy wooden benches have raised bed planters on each end, which allows me to grow grape vines on the permanent structures. They look interesting during the winter. In the summer and fall, the foliage shades the benches while I'm entertaining company. Combining containers with built-in seating will give us ample space for our large family and enough seats for everyone.

2. Meyers Lemon—Dwarf Tree

A Meyer's lemon is not quite hardy in my growing zone, so by planting this evergreen fruit tree in a large container I can bring it into a sheltered area during cold snaps. Use the largest container you can move for the healthiest plant—I'll use a colorful Mexican pot, which will bring out the colors of all the other plants on the patio. Any dwarf citrus would work here if you prefer oranges or grapefruits, but try to find a hardier variety if you're north of zone 8 or 9.

3. Nasturiums and Creeping Oregano or Marjoram— Edible Flowers and Herbs

There are four large containers in big metal watering troughs we can repurpose from my in-laws' ranch and each will be planted with layers of edibles. Mixing

Grapes need sturdy arbors, and these archways over the sitting benches are perfect for creating a shady reading nook on the patio. Photo courtesy of Alfred Diem.

Lemons bring immense interest to a patio sitting area through evergreen foliage and beautiful fruit. Photo courtesy of Liz West.

Nasturtiums are fabulous climbing or trailing edible flowers. This variety is called Night and Day. Photo courtesy of Sue St Jean, founder of www.LessNoise-MoreGreen.com

edible flowers with useful and pungent culinary herbs, like creeping oregano and creeping marjoram, will help foil pests and provide interest in the trailing habit over the edge of the container. The foliage contrast will be lovely also. See Chapter 5 for more information about Nasturtium and Chapter 7 for more information about oregano and marjoram.

4. Peas and Beans—Annual Vines

I love rotating annuals through the same space. In this case I'll plant peas for cool-season harvests in the fall through early spring, and then plant beans to follow the peas up the same trellis for warm-season harvests all summer long. Same space but

with multiple harvests. See Chapter 5 for information about growing peas, beans, and cultivars that you might want to try. Trellises can be created from simple lattice, lightweight wooden strips, or even natural twine.

5. Squash Plants—Annual Vines

Even a few bean plants will provide a robust harvest so I wanted to alternate what I grew in each container. Two of the four big trough containers will grow vining squash plants up their trellises. These vertical structures not only increase the amount of produce able to be harvested from this small space garden, but also add increased interest by displaying multiple plants at multiple levels.

FOUR CONTAINERS—MID-GROUND PLANTS

Each of the four containers will have a variety of plants growing in the middle between the trellised and edging plants. The numbers correspond to the containers in this case, not the individual plants.

6. Parsley, Arugula, and Mixed Greens

This container will provide a lot of salad greens and garnishes right when you need them. Frequent planting and harvesting of the lettuces and leafy greens will prevent them from bolting when the weather heats up. Plan to replant a section every couple weeks as you harvest them

Squash look amazing in containers—whether planted singly or in combination with other plants. Photo first appeared in *Easy Container Combos: Vegetables & Flowers* and is used courtesy of Pamela Crawford.

Swiss chard is stunning when grouped together in a planter or container. Photo courtesy of M Williams, founder of A Moveable Garden.

Tomatoes look stunning when the fruit is ripening and were originally grown for ornamental beauty only. Photo courtesy of Liz West.

and consider a shade cloth if the trellised plants don't provide enough shade to keep the greens going.

7. Swiss Chard in Mixed Colors

Swiss Chard tolerates heat a little better than many other greens, so I allow them to grow bigger before harvesting. Still this bed will get frequently harvested and may need replanting throughout the season. Swiss chard comes in a variety of colors and looks really beautiful even in ornamental settings.

8. Container Tomatoes

Three bush form plants will fit in this space. The dwarf tomatoes grow about 2–3 feet tall. I will select cherry or grape varieties that are perfect for harvesting and eating fresh. Salad at your fingertips! What could be simpler?

9. Culinary Herbs: Sage, Dill, and Lemongrass

Dill has such beautiful feathery foliage that I love using it in containers, even without an edible purpose. But with canning the summer squash that we're also growing in this container, we'll have the ability to make homemade pickles right off the back patio. Lemongrass is delicious in tea or for adding a citrus burst to salads, and can be harvested at any point in the growing season. Sage is a perennial herb and comes in a variety of colors including gray, green, and purple variegated that will contrast with dill and lemongrass beautifully.

10. Aloe Vera and Calendula

These two herbs are easy to grow and often used in wellness situations. Aloe vera is a succulent plant, grows well in a container, and is hardy to zone 8. Be prepared to give it a sunny window with winter protection if your area gets a cold snap; otherwise, little maintenance is required. The sap from the leaves is used to sooth irritated or sunburned skin. Calendula is a low-maintenance plant with beautiful orange flowers that resemble daisies. It's used in creams, lotions, salves, and teas. It will readily reseed itself in the garden, so growing in a container is one way to keep it in bounds.

11. Peppers—Annual Vegetable

I love fish peppers, a cultivar from Baker Creek Seeds. It has beautifully variegated foliage and uniquely striped peppers. Planting it in its own container will help it stand out instead of mixing it with other plants. Peppers are warm-season annuals that love plenty of sun and will produce heavily even in a container.

12. Eggplant—
Annual Warm-Season Vegetable

Another beautiful container plant, eggplant produces well in the confined space if you choose a more compact variety. Ping Tung is an heirloom variety with long, skinny fruits that range from dark purple to medium purple. Or Charming is white streaked with purple that looks ornamental and is quite productive during the summer season.

13. Giant Red Japanese Mustard

In a final small container, I will plant a really pretty leafy green that deserved to be set apart from the others—the giant red Japanese mustard. Its foliage is naturally colored from chartreuse to burgundy, providing its own color contrast. Harvest the outside leaves first while they are still tender and the plant will continue to grow with new leaves on the inside of the bunch. Ornamental, but also delicious, this is an heirloom that serves a spot in the garden.

Calendula is an easy-to-grow plant with pretty flowers. Photo courtesy of Sue St Jean, founder of www.LessNoise-MoreGreen.com

Peppers can be beautiful grown as stand-alone container plants. Photo first appeared in *Easy Container Combos: Vegetables & Flowers* and is used courtesy of Pamela Crawford.

Container Garden for Patio, Deck, or Balcony
This illustration shows only the inside corner of the design. You can adapt it as large as necessary simply by adding more containers.

Perennials vs. Annuals

Perennial plants live year after year. When I discuss a perennial plant in the growing guides, you will see a hardiness zone mentioned. However, perennials planted outside of their recommended growing zones will not survive outside and will need to be treated as annuals.

Annual plants live, reproduce, and die in a single growing season. Don't be fooled by their short-lived life, however, because annuals can have a huge benefit in the edible landscape by adding plants that grow quickly and produce fruit fast.

PATHWAY, PARKWAY, OR HELL-STRIP GARDEN DESIGN

(FULL-SUN, POLLUTION, TRAFFIC, SOIL COMPACTION)

A garden design for a driveway entry border, or parkway strip, takes some very careful planning and thoughtful considerations. Typically this area is actually owned by the city, but maintained by the homeowner. It's typically weedy grass and little else.

There are a *lot* of considerations. In fact, I recommend that while this "hell strip" can be beneficial to the edible landscape, you do not harvest edibles from it for internal consumption. The parkway strip can often contain pollutants from road traffic, pet urine, feces from wandering dogs, and anything the city sprays or street cleaners use, including salt applications in areas with winter snowfall. Any plants in this area are also combating soil compaction and likely foot traffic as well. Not to mention the fact that since the city uses this area, this should be considered a "temporary" planting. If they tear it up to dig up a water line, you don't want to lose an expensive or rare fruit tree.

So how can we make this area part of an overall edible landscape design for your home keeping all these elements in mind? Well, every good ninja story has a faithful sidekick and this area will play a huge supporting role to the rest of your garden area. We will plant nectary and insectory plants—plants that attract beneficial insects to the area and help your other garden plants as a result.

> *"The hum of bees is the voice of the garden."*
> —Elizabeth Lawrence

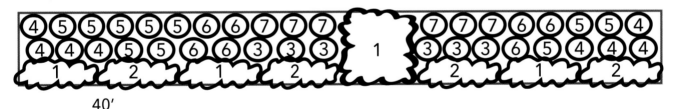

40'

1. Creeping Thyme
2. Sweet Alyssum – Summer Peaches
3. Yarrow – Summer Pastels
4. Cosmos – Sonata Mix
5. Echinacea – Paradise Mix
6. Zinnia – Candy Stripe Mix
7. Anise Hyssop – Golden Jubilee

PLANTS FOR THE HELL-STRIP

Bees, hummingbirds, and butterflies benefit many garden plants, especially in an edible design. Your garden will profit from the hardy, colorful, long-lasting flowers in this extra space. And your garden will win because of it. This design assumes a full-sun area, but if you're planting near a tree, I will give you some dappled shade alternatives to consider as substitutes.

1. Creeping Thyme (*Thymus pulegiodes*)— Semi-Evergreen Ground Cover

You already know from my other designs how much I love this beautiful ground-cover herb. Here's your chance to plant it where it really shines—in full sun. It's tolerant of light foot traffic; put this herb where car doors will hit it or where neighbor children tend to cut through, and it will bounce back faster than other ground covers. Plant in drifts to lead the eye.

2. Sweet Alyssum (*Lobularia maritima*)—Annual

This flowering annual is a powerhouse at attracting pollinators to the garden. It's a butterfly and honeybee magnet, and the flowers will last for months. Sweetly fragrant and available in a wide variety of colors, sweet alyssum goes great with thyme ground cover. Use any of the ground covers from the Part Shade Foundation Planter as substitutes or consider something like *lamium* or *sedum ellacombianum*, which has bright yellow flowers.

3. Yarrow (*Achillea millefolium*)—Perennial

This gorgeous flowering perennial is hardy in zones 3–9. There are dozens of color options available and sizes range from 1–4 feet. The clusters of flowers bloom throughout the summer and fall and attract a wide variety of pollinators to the garden area. For this design, I will choose a shorter variety that stays around 2–3 feet tall to allow for line of sight to the road.

4. Cosmos (*Cosmos bipinnatus*)— Annual

These charming flowers will look good under pressure, no doubt about it. Sprinkle the seeds around just after your last frost date in spring and enjoy cheerful, daisy-like flowers for months. Since cosmos can become too leggy and thin-stemmed in overly rich soil, the poor soil of the parkway strip will actually keep them thriving. Choose a color that complements your design preferences and combines well with your other plants.

This alyssum is a 1953 All-America Selection winner called Royal Carpet, and it's popular to this day. Alyssum is available in many colors. Photo courtesy of All-America Selections.

My friend Teri has this lovely herb and flower border near her vegetable garden to attract pollinators to her garden. Yarrow in the foreground mixes well with the chives, echinacea, and other herbs. Photo courtesy of Teri Page of Homestead Honey.

5. Purple Coneflower (*Echinacea*)— Perennial

Despite the common name, echinacea is actually widely hybridized and available in several colors—purple to mauve to orange spectrum especially. I chose smaller cultivars so they would be only 2–3 feet tall and maintain good visibility to the road. Echinacea is a perennial, so it may be slower to start in the spring but will provide weeks of flowers through the summer and fall.

6. Zinnia—Annual

Another great plant to start from seed, the zinnia is a favorite of children because the seeds are easy to plant and bloom so quickly. They typically don't transplant well, like cosmos, so are easiest to start from seed. I chose a named cultivar with colors that would complement the overall design. Like most of the flowering plants in this design,

I love the warm, vibrant color of this AAS winner, PowWow Wildberry. Photo courtesy of All-America Selections.

Swap out full-sun or mostly-sun choices like the yarrow, cosmos, and zinnia for these annuals and perennials that will attract pollinators to a shady space.

Bee Balm (Monarda)

Astilbe

Hosta

Columbine

Coral Bells (Heuchera)

Blue Star (Amsonia)

Woodland Phlox (Phlox divaricata)

Blue Mistflower (Conoclinium coelestinum)

these flowers attract pollinators and make excellent cutting flowers for indoor flower arrangements.

7. Anise Hyssop (*Agastache foeniculum*)—Perennial Herb

A great, free flowering plant for attracting pollinators, anise hyssop makes an excellent addition to a mixed bed or border. It is drought tolerant and has beautiful purple flower spikes and attractive arrow-shaped leaves. The flower spikes contrast in form with some of the other, more rounded flowers. They are 2–3 feet tall so well-suited to this space.

As you can see, the limitations and challenges faced by trying to plant the parkway strip can be overcome simply by changing your focus. If you decide to use this space for plants that attract pollinators and house beneficial insects, it becomes easier. If your parkway strip is wider than my sample design, you could potentially grow edibles in raised beds or containers but should expect to lose some to passers-by.

Zinnias are easily grown from seed and have blooms that last for months. Photo courtesy of Missouri Botanical Garden

Parkway Pollinator Garden Design

This design allows a great deal of flexibility in terms of length and width to fit any space that you want to fill.

A border of cut flowers and pollinators will bring beneficial insects to the area. Photos courtesy of Liz West.

Pollinator Border Along Roadside—Full Sun, High Traffic

This border allows for some visual distance between a road and the homeowner's front yard. The border ties right into the yard for a wildflower, prairie-style look. Yet the gorgeous flowers bring pollinators to the property, create visual interest, and create a sense of screening from the passing motorists. Many of the flowers could also be used as cut flowers for wildflower arrangements as well! It's a great use of otherwise hard-to-mow and wasted space.

SMALL SPACE SIDE YARD

(FULL SUN AND SCREENING NEEDED)

This side yard gives the opportunity for a small space border that follows the line of the house. With the need for getting a lawn mower past the side of the house or walking from front to back, the bed of this side yard can't be too wide. To further complicate this garden design, this is the space where the large AC unit sits, so plants will offer some screening of the unit without overgrowing it. We need mounding plants that won't grow over the windows, or destroy the siding, yet will create interest and be useful, and will tolerate pruning around the AC unit for regular maintenance in the off season. This area is also full sun.

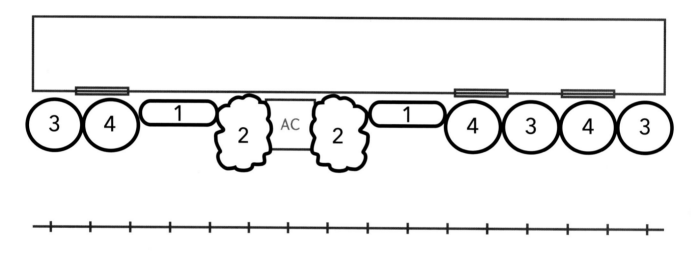

1. Currant – Red Currant, trained as espalier
2. Goji Berries – Sweet Lifeberry
3. Rosemary – Tuscan Blue
4. Borage

---

1. **Currant** (*Ribes*)— Fruitful Vine or Bush

Currants are self-fruitful vines or rambling shrubs that can be easily trained along a fence or wall. In this small space, I will train them on the wall between the windows in espalier form for easy access and harvesting. They are hardy in zones 3–7, so in my area they may need some summer protection. They will also benefit from having the borage planted around its feet and the shade that will be cast by the goji bushes screening the AC unit. The flowers hang in pretty clusters like strands of pearls, and the summer fruit is also lovely.

2. **Goji Berry** (*Lycium barbarum*)— Fruiting Shrub

These open, fruitful shrubs produce pretty red berries called goji berries. Not as commonly grown in home gardens, there are now named cultivars that produce sweeter berries or larger berries than the goji plants. Sweet Lifeberry by Proven Winners has sweeter-than-average berries and the loose, open habit of the plants makes them good for a living screen. Tie the canes together and use simple bamboo stakes to help support the plants and make harvesting easier. It also tolerates pruning extremely well—even in the middle of the growing season—making it easy for us to get to the unit any time the AC needs to be worked on.

3. **Rosemary** (*Rosmarinus officinalis*)— Perennial Woody Herb

One of my favorite herbs, this plant just continues from the side of the foundation planting (that I shared earlier in this chapter) and wraps around the side of the house. It's easy to harvest sprigs for use on the grill, and the evergreen foliage looks great year round against the brick. The upright growth contrasts nicely with goji's open form and the horizontal training we're doing with the currants. Since this rosemary is planted in the ground rather than a container I'll use an upright form like Tuscan Blue or Spice Islands.

4. **Borage** (*Borago officinalis*)— Perennial Herb

Filling in the gaps between the rosemary, windows, and around the currants will be a far-too-overlooked herb: borage. I love these pretty blue flowers, and their tolerance for soil that isn't as good in quality and their large gray-green leaves. Their foliage will contrast with rosemary well. The plant is highly useful as well. Their leaves are used in soups, stews, and salads, and the flowers make an excellent garnish or flavoring in tea or lemonade.

Red currants produce delicious soft berries like strings of pearls. Photo courtesy of Liz West.

Goji berries are shrubs with a loose growing habit, perfect for a natural screen. Photo courtesy of Proven Winners.

This may seem like a simple design, but it's well suited to this space, makes good use of otherwise wasted areas around the house, and solves the problem of the AC eye-sore that would otherwise be visible from the road when people drive up to the house. Plus we now have beautiful flowers and plants visible through the windows of the bedrooms, and everything is dressed up a lot more. By continuing plants from the front foundation planter around the side, we also create a sense of continuity for the entire house.

This side yard is small, but filled with gorgeous and productive plants arranged beautifully to produce as many fruits as possible. Photo courtesy of Alfred Diem.

Small Space Side Yard Garden

Combining screening plants to hide eyesores like ACs or trash cans, with repeated elements like the perennials, makes it easy to adapt this design to any sized side yard.

Foliage contrasts are important in the garden. They help hold interest and let each plant stand out as the rock star that it is. Sometimes that contrast is in the shape and size of the foliage rather than the color of the foliage, as seen with this rosemary and borage combination I've included in this design. Here are some other edible plant foliage contrasts to consider.

Broad Foliage		*Fine Foliage*	
Sage	Chard	Dianthus	Chamomile
Nasturtium	Ginger	Dill	Ginger
Tuberous Begonia	Pepper	Chives	Sweet Woodruff
Lemon Balm		Lemon Grass	Oregano

The contrast between kale's bold foliage and the fine, lacy foliage of dill, is stunning. Photo courtesy of M. Williams, Founder of A Moveable Garden.

Photos by Angie Runyan

Angie Runyan
Illinois, Zone 5

Productive Side yard

We grow a stand of raspberries planted between a garage and an alley in what would otherwise be wasted space. These bushes produce like crazy every year for me. I keep meaning to measure amounts, but we're too busy eating them to determine how much we produce. I did just make twelve 8-ounce jars of jelly with the berries, still have about 6–8 cups left to eat. Previous to making the jelly, we probably harvested about 15–20 cups of berries—all from a skinny little space only about 20 feet x 3 feet.

I have mixed responses from my neighbors. Some like to snatch a few raspberries on occasion. The garbage man picks a few here and there. One neighbor with a neighboring garage was worried about the bushes scratching his car and so used pesticide to limit their growth on that end of the stand. The few near there that survived the assault produced strangely shaped berries. I guess my offering of a bowl of berries wasn't enough to change his perspective. Maybe a copy of your book would help. :)

FRUIT AND HERB CORNER IN BACKYARD

(FULL SUN MULTI-LEVEL PLANTS)

Creating a fruit tree and herb corner in your backyard gives you the opportunity to create your own miniature woodland environment. By layering the taller trees, medium shrubs, and then smaller herbs and ground covers below that you create a mini-ecosystem full of beneficial insects and less likely to spread disease than a monoculture environment. Plus, it looks pretty!

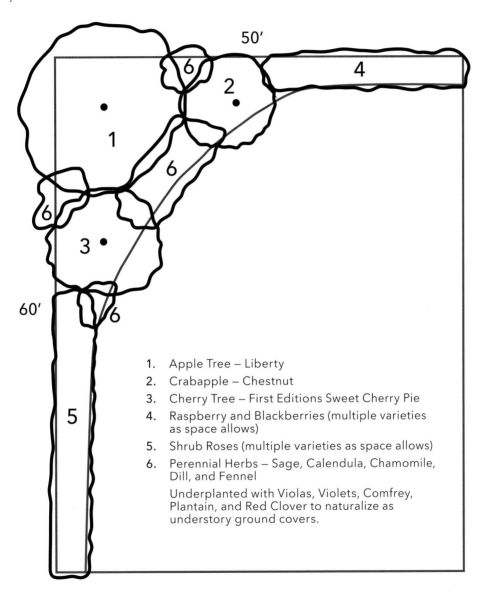

1. Apple Tree – Liberty
2. Crabapple – Chestnut
3. Cherry Tree – First Editions Sweet Cherry Pie
4. Raspberry and Blackberries (multiple varieties as space allows)
5. Shrub Roses (multiple varieties as space allows)
6. Perennial Herbs – Sage, Calendula, Chamomile, Dill, and Fennel

   Underplanted with Violas, Violets, Comfrey, Plantain, and Red Clover to naturalize as understory ground covers.

A mature apple tree with craggy bark against the stunning spring blooms is a gorgeous show worth adding to your landscape. Photo courtesy of Liz West.

This small cherry tree is gorgeous in bloom beside tansy in this edible backyard bed. Photo courtesy of M. Williams, Founder of A Moveable Garden.

1. Apple Tree

The Liberty apple is extremely disease resistant, making it a good choice for an organic home garden spot. Apples are generally hardy in zones 4–7, and you can check for varieties resistant to diseases most common in your area with your local extension office. Grown on semi-dwarf rootstock, Liberty will reach about 15 feet tall and wide, and serve as the focal point for this fruit border. It needs a pollinator, however, so one of the two smaller trees will be a crabapple, which is not only edible, but also a great pollinator for this apple. Be sure if you choose a different apple cultivar, that you make sure you plant is a suitable pollinator for it.

2. Chestnut Crabapple

This crabapple is one of the best for producing edible fruits. The crabapples are a larger than average crabapples (especially the ornamental varieties typically available in nursery centers and big box stores). The tree will grow about 10–12 feet tall and wide, and has gorgeous white blooms in the spring. See more about how to grow apples in Chapter 6.

3. Cherry Tree

Since I only plan to have one cherry tree in this garden design, I will choose a self-pollinating variety like Sweet Cherry Pie from Bailey Nursery. If you choose to plant two cherries instead of two apples, choose cultivars that cross-pollinate. Cherries have incredible flowers, and this cultivar has a vibrant rosy-pink color. The cherries are sweet enough to eat fresh without being too sweet for pies and cobblers. Naturally semi-dwarfed, this tree reaches about 12–15 feet, perfect for this space.

4. Raspberry and Blackberry Border

Brambles make such great hedges that it only makes sense to include them in a space like this. Let them grow against the back fence, and choose your cultivars according to your needs. If it's an area where you often walk or you want to make picking your berries easier, choose thornless varieties. If you want to create more of a barrier, use thorned varieties. Raspberries and blackberries epitomize the taste of summer to me, but they are almost impossible to get from the store because they bruise easily in shipping. These plants are easy to grow and are usually highly productive, so plant as many as the space allows.

5. Shrub Roses

Roses are edible flowers and look amazing in the landscape. If you choose roses that produce attractive rose hips, you'll get twice the benefit. They have summer flowers, have winter interest, and are useful fruits. Rose hips are high in vitamin C and can be dehydrated and used in winter teas. I love the old-fashioned look and modern disease hardiness of the David Austin roses. For this design I'll choose a cultivar that has beautiful rose hips and amazing fragrance, like Scepter'd Isle. It's hardy, highly fragrant, and blooms constantly throughout the summer. It won't stop there, however, because you'll have rose hips for interest come winter.

We grew these thornless blackberries over simple wooden sawhorses to help screen the chain link fence in our front yard. They bore a huge amount of fruit even in their first year. Amazing!

When selecting shrub roses for an edible landscape, choose a rose that will produce ample hips like this Scepter'd Isle rose. Photo courtesy of David Austin Roses.

Sage is a great herb for interplanting among other trees, shrubs, perennials, and annuals. It's lovely texture and color tones usually play well with other plants in the landscape. Photo courtesy of Missouri Botanical Garden.

6. Herb Understory

In between the drip lines of the trees where there are sunnier open spots is a great space for pretty herbs. Choose herbs that flower for prolonged periods in the summer and fall, or have attractive foliage, to complement the fruit trees well. I will choose sage, calendula, chamomile, dill, and fennel. Other herbs you might try are tansy, feverfew, yarrow, or hyssop.

7. Ground Covers

Around and under the trees and shrubs you can plant a ground cover of herbs and edible flowers. Violas and violets are perfect for the shadier nooks, and red clover will help fix nitrogen in the sunnier spots. Both are lovely ground covers that won't compete too much for the resources the fruit trees need. Taller herbs for this space include comfrey, plantain, and sorrel.

It seems like a simple, small space that runs along the fence lines and takes only one corner of the backyard. But this garden will produce bushels of fruit each year for you and your family.

Violets can form an attractive ground cover. Photo courtesy of Liz West.

"Autumn is the mellower season and what we lose in flowers we more than gain in fruits."

—Samuel Butler

Fruit and Herb Corner

This design transforms a drab corner into a fruitful space. The roses on the left and
the raspberries on the right can continue as far as space and desire allow.

THREE-SEASON ISLAND

(FULL SUN, MULTI-SEASON INTEREST)

Sometimes you just want an area that you can play with and really create something to show off your favorite plants. That's what this Three-Season Island is for me. This island planter takes more maintenance than some of my other designs. Switching out containers, planting annuals for warm-season harvests, and then succession planting for cool-season color, and so on, takes a lot of work. But it becomes a really pretty showpiece area for my garden. I show the planter in spring, summer, and fall so you can see how the seasonal fluctuations affect your garden design and outcome.

SPRING IN THE THREE-SEASON ISLAND

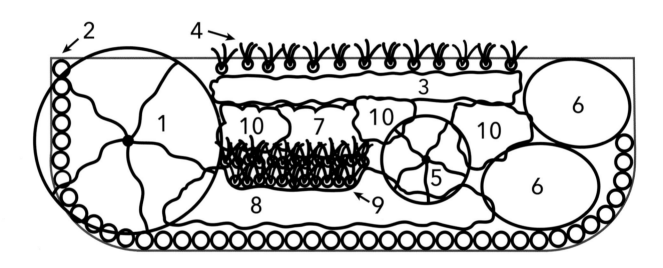

1. Persimmon
2. Lettuce
3. Asparagus
4. Tulips – Greuze or Madras
5. Bonfire Peach (in large container)
6. Sweetberry Honeysuckle
7. Primrose
8. Violas mixed
9. Daffodils – Daphne
10. Columbine

1. Persimmon—Fruit Tree

Believe it or not, this fruit tree isn't the show-stopper in spring that the other fruits will be. But persimmons have an interesting look year-round and have attractive leaves.

2. Lettuce—Cool-Season Annual

The entire edge border of the planter will be planted in lettuce or cabbage for mounded, foliage-focused edging. You can either mix lettuces for a variety of colors or use the same variety all the way across the border.

3. Asparagus—Perennial Vegetable

Asparagus shoots are ready for harvesting first thing in the spring, as soon as they begin to appear. Harvest shoots that are thick as a pencil or larger, before the tips unfurl. Leave shoots that are thinner than a regular pencil, so that they can grow, develop into fronds, and give the plant energy for the following year. In this season they won't be visible until you go looking for the shoots to harvest.

4. Tulips—Spring-Blooming Bulbs

I will interplant the asparagus with large, early tulips. This gives me bright swaths of color where I don't otherwise have any interest. Once the tulips are spent, the asparagus fronds will be growing up and disguising the spent foliage of the bulbs. Since tulips can naturalize well, I don't anticipate replanting them and disturbing the asparagus roots on a regular basis. I love Greuze, a deep purple heirloom tulip that grows 2 feet tall. Old House Gardens also has a tulip called Madras, another heirloom that has a cool coppery color and can be over 2 feet tall.

5. Peach—Container Fruit Tree

In a large container plant is a dwarf peach. Bonfire is a gorgeous peach tree with

"My garden is my most beautiful masterpiece."
—Claude Monet

Lettuce makes a lovely edging plant in a mixed bed or border. Plant a mix of colors for a more informal feel. Photo courtesy of Jeannie Sanders.

The early spring foliage of this Bonfire Peach is highly ornamental. Courtesy of Brandy Hopper.

Violas are a gorgeous, cheerful, edible spring flower. Photo courtesy of Missouri Botanical Garden.

burgundy foliage and deeper pink flowers. It is highly attractive in the spring with sprays of incredible blooms. The fruit isn't large enough to eat out of hand, like a traditional peach tree, but can be harvested for preserves or cobblers. This is one of those cases where the balance between ornamental and edible swayed me toward those incredible purple leaves.

6. Sweetberry Honeysuckles (*Lonicera caerula*)—Shrubs

These pretty, informal shrubs bear fruit in the summer, but for now their early growth is attractive enough to easily earn them a spot in this border.

The rest of the design is filled with cool-season perennials that have edible blooms or shoots—except the daffodils. They are not edible but they sure are pretty and complement the other spring blooms in the design.

7. Primrose

Primrose are edible plants with cheerful clumps of flowers atop a wreath of leaves. The entire plant generally stays well-behaved in the garden area. The leaves are used as potherbs in soups and stews, while the flowers are used to season teas and syrups. Enjoy their spring show while they are blooming and choose a variety with a color that will complement the bulbs you chose.

8. Violas—Cool-Season Perennials

In my area, these gorgeous flowers often die in the hottest days of summer, but if they've had time to bloom and set seed, they will be back. Violas and sweet violets are in the same family and the flowers are edible. Different colors have different flavors and the bluer ones taste the best to me. Enjoy these fragrant ground covers while they last. I sprinkle the seeds generously all over the area I want them to grow in the fall and let them find their own favorite places to grow from there.

9. Daffodil—Spring-Blooming Bulb

Another spring blooming bulb, but this one is not edible. It is, however, completely gorgeous. Somehow it doesn't seem like spring without some daffodils. I'm planning to use a large, heirloom variety called Daphne that will reach almost 2 feet tall. They are planted where the chamomile will grow come summer so as the daffodil's foliage dies back, the chamomile will help disguise it.

10. Columbine—Perennial Flower

Cheerful early blooms on graceful stems, columbine is a short-lived perennial in my area. I like to plant them though, for their early shade flowers and the pretty clover-like foliage. If you're in a cooler-summer area than my 100 degrees, you will have better luck and might not have to resow seeds every 2–3 years. They give great cool-season color for later winter color, but they will melt away by summer when my sage and annual veggies take over the space.

"I love Spring everywhere, but if I could choose I would always greet it in a garden."

—Ruth Stout

Three-Season Island in Spring
Spring allows the flowers and shrubs to take center stage.

SUMMER IN THE THREE-SEASON ISLAND

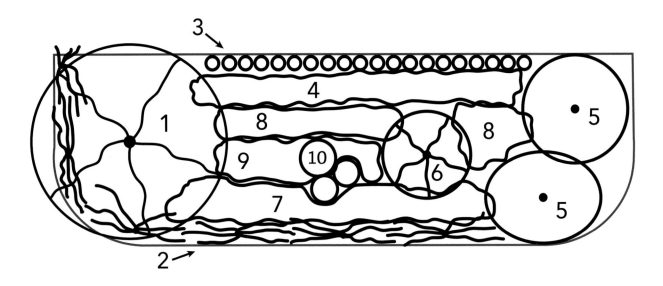

1. Persimmon Tree
2. Squash
3. Summer sunflowers
4. Asparagus
5. Sweetberry Honeysuckle
6. Bonfire Peach
7. Feverfew
8. Sage – multiple types
9. Chamomile
10. Peppers or Purple Okra

1. Persimmon

Now summer foliage is completely grown out and looks beautiful. Plants under the densest part of the tree won't have as much sunlight but still receive part sun throughout the day. The fruits may be just visible by late summer but persimmon's months of glory have not yet arrived.

2. Squash

Lettuce often cannot tolerate the heat of summer, although some may be able to grow year round under the persimmon tree where temperatures are more moderate in the shade. The squash vines will take over the lettuce as a trailing, vining edging plant. Plant squash every 5 or 6 feet along the edge of the planter and then train the vines along the edge and toward the other squash plants to fill in the gaps. It's a little more work but squash usually has large leaves and looks really cool as a temporary, summer ground cover.

3. Summer Sunflowers

Planted as soon as the danger of frost was over, these sunflowers are rapidly growing plants already in bloom. Choose a variety that will bloom in early summer, and interplant this space with a fall-blooming variety. Your summer plants are in full bloom, and your fall sunflowers are still green and growing up in between them. Their leggy growth is disguised by the asparagus ferns.

4. Asparagus—Perennial Vegetable

Asparagus in summer is a gorgeous, ferny plant with leafy fronds. In this case, they serve as an airy backdrop for the flowering herbs and help soften the leggy stems of the sunflowers. Any bulb foliage still dying will also be hidden. Win-win-win!

5. Sweetberry Honeysuckle—Shrub

Sweetberry honeysuckle can be pretty shrubby but has attractive foliage and delicious fruit. This shrub is already setting fruit in the summer, so watch it carefully for signs of ripeness. The blue berries are highly nutritious and have a lot of antioxidants. Fruit holds well on the shrub during ripening so harvest in batches and freeze extras to use in smoothies and desserts later in the year. I included two in this garden design because they bear fruit better with cross-pollination.

6. Bonfire Peach

The peach will now be in full leaf and setting small fruit. Flowering season over, the peach is still extremely attractive and stands out beautifully in front of the asparagus background. Purple foliage contrasts nicely with yellow sunflowers.

7. Feverfew and 9. Chamomile—Flowering Perennial Herbs

Chamomile and feverfew both have daisy-like flowers and will quickly burst into bloom. Expect flowers to last for weeks

This vining cucumber is being used as an annual ground cover for this mixed border. Love it! Photo courtesy of M Williams, founder of A Moveable Garden.

Asparagus won't be uniform all the way through the harvest period. Stop harvesting when they are pencil-thin. Photo courtesy of Liz West.

Lonicera, or sweetberry honeysuckle, produces delicious and edible summer fruit. Photo courtesy of Proven Winners.

This heirloom okra Jing Orange is more colorful during the summer growing season than many that are typically found in the big box stores. Photo courtesy of Baker Creek Seeds.

through summer and on into the fall. Both plants make good cutting flower filler or can be dehydrated to use in tea blends.

8. Sage

There are several kinds of sages with different colored foliage, and I plan to include a couple different types here. Gray-leafed sage and tricolor sage look particularly good together in my opinion. The purple in tricolor sage will pick up the burgundy of the bonfire peach. The primroses and violas that were in this space have probably set their seed by now and will welcome the shade of the sage during as the days heat up.

10. Peppers or Okra— Annual Vegetables

Both ornamental and useful, a purple or red foliage vegetable plant would be perfect here. Okra and peppers both have cultivars that would work well, and as total sun-lovers they will do beautifully during the dog days of summer. The violas that were here are either no more or turning lanky so they don't feel bad that I've transplanted these vegetables here. Try Jing Orange or Red Velvet okra or Emerald Fire or Super Chili peppers for colored vegetable bushes that will create some nice interest in this space.

Three-Season Island in Summer
The foliage of summer is lush and beautiful, while summer flowers and herbs create spotlights of color throughout.

FALL IN THE THREE-SEASON ISLAND

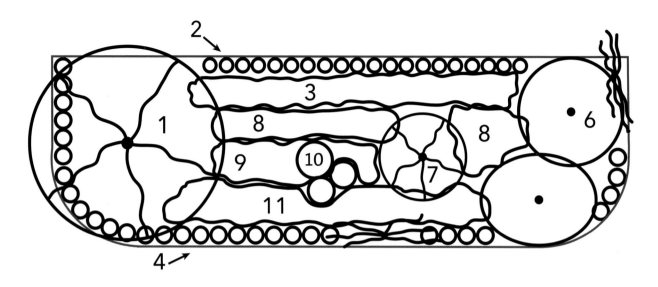

1. Persimmon
2. Sunflowers with fall blooms
3. Asparagus
4. Lettuce (mixed colors)
5. Squash
   (remove spent vines and interplant
   Lettuce as Squash is harvested)

6. Sweetberry Honeysuckle
7. Bonfire Peach
8. Sage
9. Chamomile
10. Kale
11. Feverfew

1. Persimmon

And now our persimmon steps up into the spotlight with large orange fruit born on strong, spreading limbs. Persimmons hold their fruit long into fall and even winter in some areas, because the fruits are not fully ripe until after first frost. One of my favorite gardening moments was our persimmon in our Texas home covered in snow and still holding bright orange fruit.

2. Sunflowers

Now fall sunflowers are in full bloom and bring russets and copper tones to the mix instead of the pure yellow of summer's flowers. The sunflowers will help support the asparagus ferns, which can be more susceptible to being blown over in fall storms. We want the asparagus to store as much energy as possible before winter's cold kills the fronds. We want to have a good harvest in the spring.

3. Asparagus

Let the fronds continue to grow as long as possible. We typically don't cut them back until well into winter when all the foliage dies back with winter's frost.

4. Lettuce

A mix of greens and reds would be welcome with the other fall colors we have in the garden. I love the heirloom varieties with their unique speckled looks and intriguing names. Sow seeds around the squash vines in late summer, and they will naturally grow into place as temperatures cool off. Trim back the squash vines once the lettuce has grown large enough to take over the job of edging plant. Easy peasy!

5. Squash

Remove any spent vines. If you have winter squashes that are still finishing their maturation, it won't be too much longer before you've harvested all of them.

6. Sweetberry Honeysuckle

These shrubs will give a surprising amount of color in the fall landscape, while holding their leaves nicely until frost sets in. If they are done fruiting, you can prune lightly after the third or fourth year. Berries form on old-wood, so don't over prune.

7. Bonfire Plum

The bonfire plum will be finished fruiting now and may turn colors for the fall depending on your climate. It's a total workhorse in the landscape!

Persimmons take the stage in the fall, and sometimes into winter, with their brilliant fruit. Photo courtesy of Amy Lenzo, Founder of BeautyDialogues.com.

Different sunflowers have different bloom times. Stagger them for a long-lasting season. Photo courtesy of Sue St Jean, founder of www.LessNoise-MoreGreen.com

8. Sage, 9. Chamomile, and 11. Feverfew

Allow these flowers to continue to bloom well into fall. Chamomile and feverfew might sow their own seeds and produce volunteer plants in the following year!

10. Kale and Cabbage

Replace the cold-sensitive annual vegetables with hardier choices like kale and cabbage. Choose different colors and shapes for more visual interest.

And there you have it—a really fun, ever-changing island that will always give you something to do. Whether it's harvesting fresh asparagus straight from the garden, training a squash vine in the right direction, or testing your persimmons for ripeness in the fall, you'll always have a reason to wander through this garden during your morning cup of coffee. Enjoy the cyclical shifts of the seasons and see how each month brings its own beauty to forefront.

"All gardening is landscape painting, said Alexander Pope."

—Rebecca Solnit

A border of edible greens can be very attractive in a fall garden. Photo by Paul Straatman, courtesy of Missouri Botanical Garden.

Three-Season Island in Fall

Fall allows our fruit tree to take the stage while russets and oranges fill the rest of the border with color.

PART III

Plants That Matter

The plants are absolutely the keys to crafting a brilliant edible landscape. They are the building blocks you use to build your beautiful bounty. In this part you'll not only learn how to grow certain kinds of plants, but also find some recommendations for specific varieties and cultivars that have particular star-power in the landscape.

WHAT YOU'LL FIND:

Botanical Info – Each entry will be sorted alphabetically by common name. You will find the basic botanical information, the scientific name, and hardiness zones where applicable.

Growing Guide – You'll find information about how to grow the plant, maintenance notes for basic care, and any tips for utilizing it in the landscape.

Potential Pests and Diseases – This section will highlight types of pests that may be attracted to this plant, as well as common diseases to watch for.

How to Use – This section will tell you ways the plant may be used in the kitchen, herbal preparations, or for practical purposes in the home.

Recommendations – Here you'll find some variety and cultivar recommendations. This will only be the surface of the iceberg of possibilities. The design section (Part 2) will help you understand the thought process of how you can go from many options to picking just the right plant for the right space.

If you still need further help, join the Garden Ninjas group by going to http://UntrainedHousewife.com/GardeningLikeANinja.

I've broken these chapters up by plant usage in the landscape rather than "Perennials and Annuals" or "Fruits and Herbs." I'm allowing you the ability to more easily mix your planters this way. You'll find Vines and Ground Covers, Trees and Shrubs, and Edible Ornamental Plants, which will cover the variety of planting levels and uses.

5 From the Ground Up — Vines and Ground Covers

Vines are the icing on the landscaping cake. They fill the gaps with vertical height or rambling foliage underneath and around other plants in your beds. Sometimes vines can be allowed to lie on the ground as a ground cover, or trained and trellised to climb a vertical element. They also look great draped over the edge of raised beds, containers, or tiered planters.

These rattlesnake beans show some of the variation that is available when you explore heirloom varieties. Photo courtesy of M. Williams, Founder of A Moveable Garden.

✿ Beans

Many common beans (*P. vulga ris*) come in both pole and bush forms. Short bush forms could form a larger ground cover, but my favorites are the pole beans. They are so fun to tuck into garden design corners, near woody shrubs or small trees, in containers with wooden trellises, and along fence lines.

BOTANICAL INFORMATION: *Annual*

There are many types of beans and they aren't all in the same family; however, I'll describe all of the climbing varieties here.

- Beans, Pole and Bush (*Phaseolus vulgaris*)
- Scarlet Runner Beans (*Phaseolus coccineus*)
- Lima Beans (*Phaseolus lunatas*)
- Long Beans (*Vigna unquiculata* var. *sesquipedalis*)
- Asparagus Bean or Winged Bean (*Psophocarpus tetragonolobus*)
- Garbanzo beans (*Cicer arietinum*) (See Chapter 7)
- Fava Bean (*Vicia faba*) (See Chapter 7)

GROWING GUIDE

All of these beans (except fava, see Chapter 7) grow best in full sun. They typically will not germinate well until the ground temperature is above 50 degrees, so plant after the weather warms in the spring. They are easy to plant because the seeds are large and easy to handle. Plant beans about 2 inches deep and space them 5–12 inches apart depending on cultivar (seed packets) will have specific recommendations). I tend to plant intensively when I'm growing them upright on vertical elements.

If this is your first time growing beans in that space, I recommend using an inoculant, which you can get from a garden nursery. It will boost the plant's ability to fix nitrogen from the air into the soil. Dip your seeds into the powder (don't worry, it's organic!) and then plant the seeds. If harvesting for pods, you'll have beans ready to pick within 8–12 weeks, while dried beans take longer since the pods dry on the vine.

Beans are fabulous additions to a sunny edible garden space. Their climbing nature means they don't take too much space, and the flowers are very lovely. Even edible vines have flowers nearly as ornamental as those varieties traditionally relegated to the vegetable plot. Scarlet runner beans have bright red flowers and are a personal favorite.

Long beans tend to tolerate heat very well in general, because they are related to cow peas. Asparagus beans (also called winged beans) on the other hand tend to do better in the coastal areas and zones with shorter summer days. They have a great flavor and unique appearance, though, so are worth trying.

POTENTIAL PESTS AND DISEASES

Aphids can be a pest, as well as red spider mites, both of which can be treated organically with insecticidal soap sprayed on the leaves. Be sure to spray the underside of the leaves where the pests like to hide. Attracting beneficial insects like ladybugs is also really helpful. Mexican bean beetles can attack bean plants and eat lacey patterns in the leaves, depleting the amount of energy the plant can produce. These pests overwinter in leafy debris. Keeping an active compost bin where you break down the garden waste will help break their life cycle.

HOW TO USE

Beans are generally used for their edible pods or their edible seeds, depending on which type you're growing. Winged beans are also known to have edible shoots, and the young vines can be cooked like spinach. My favorite way to eat fresh snap peas is with the whole pods. Just snap off the ends and sauté lightly with butter and minced garlic. Harvest the young pods frequently, even daily, to keep the vines producing more flowers and pods. We usually put dried beans in our winter stew or chili. Harvest these after the pods are completely dry. Remember, the vine will stop producing new pods once the first pods begin to reach maturity.

RECOMMENDATIONS

Of course I love Scarlet Runner for the bright red blooms. Many pole beans have amazing colors and looks to contribute to the garden as well. Blue Coco is a French heirloom that has attractive blue-purple bean pods, and it does well in heat and drought conditions. Montezuma Red or Mexican Red is grown as a dried bean and has yummy dark red beans on cool sprawling vine. Chinese Red Noodle is a cool heirloom vine I found at Baker Creek Seeds. It has long, bright red pods that look great hanging down through an arbor or archway. *Trionfo Violetta* is a stunning purple podded heirloom from Italy with deep purple flowers and burgundy stems and pods. It's lovely but less heat tolerant than others. Italian Rose is a lovely heirloom that has cranberry-rose colored pods marbled with white variegation and delicious flavor.

✿ Blueberry, Lowbush (*Viburnum angustifolium*)

Blueberries as a ground cover? Absolutely!

BOTANICAL INFORMATION: *Perennial*

This plant is hardy in zones 3–7, although some areas report hardiness to zone 2. It is a self-pollinator that does better with cross-pollination, so for the best fruiting, plant multiple plants.

GROWING GUIDE

Lowbush blueberry makes an attractive, woody ground cover under shrubs or trees, although it doesn't smother weeds as completely as other ground covers. It is the perfect ground cover choice for other acid-loving plants like camellias. It looks great year-round, and it needs very little maintenance. Lowbush tolerates up to part shade, but fruits best in dappled shade to a more full sun.

Plant already-started lowbush blueberries in the fall or early spring, and amend the soil if needed to create the proper acidity level. If your soil is more alkaline than the 4.5–5.5 pH blueberries prefer, dig a larger-than-needed hole, and fill in the extra space with a mix of soil made for acidic soil-loving plants. Or create your own with peat moss, pine needles, chopped oak leaves, and so on. These blueberries will spread via underground runners and suckers to fill in the gaps between your starts over the next couple years.

Maintenance is simple. If you want the best fruit production, prune your lowbush blueberries by half each year as the plants bear fruit best on year-old shoots. If you prune all the plants at once, you'll set back your fruit production. Blueberries are very shallow-rooted so the biggest danger would be allowing them to dry out. Use acidic mulch like chopped oak leaves or pine needles to help preserve water. Test and amend the soil once a year as needed to keep the acidity level where it needs to be, and your blueberries will probably be happy campers.

Blueberries have lovely spring flowers, deep green foliage, and lovely fall color. Harvest the berries when they are totally ripe in mid-to-late summer and eat! You will know when they are ripe because they will easily fall into your hand. You'll have to move quickly to beat the birds though. Planting them close by the house can help prevent some of this predation.

POTENTIAL PESTS AND DISEASES

This blueberry has very few, if any, pests and diseases as long as the soil has the proper acidity level.

HOW TO USE

Wow! When it comes to blueberries the better question is how not to use? Blueberries can be made into jellies and syrups, added fresh to smoothies, pancakes, and baked goods, or added dried to cereal and granola. They will store fresh in the fridge (when washed and fully dried) for about five days, or you can freeze them for about six months. They also dehydrate easily for long-term storage as well. Blueberries represent my favorite kind of edibles—delicious flavor and amazing nutritional value.

RECOMMENDATIONS

Lowbush blueberries don't typically come in a lot of named cultivars but are hybridized easily. Buying from a regional grower means you'll get starts that are probably well-adapted to your local area.

✿ Cucumbers—see Squash in this chapter

Grapes need a sturdy support since they are heavy, perennial fruit-bearing vines. Photo courtesy of Alfred Diem.

✿ Grapes (*Vitis* spp.)

BOTANICAL INFORMATION: *Perennial*

- American or Fox grape (*Vitis labrusca*) are hardy in zones 3–7.
- European grapes (*Vitis vinifera*) are hardy in zones 7–10, although select varieties have been bred for more cold tolerance.
- Muscadine grapes (*Vitis rotundifolia*) are hardy in zones 7–9.

American hybrids are generally crosses between the *V. Labrusca* and *V. Vinifera* in order to increase cold-hardiness of vineyard, fruitful vines. These hybrids typically fall in hardiness zones around 5–10.

GROWING GUIDE

Grapes fruit best in full sun. When grown as companions with fruit trees, they grow all the way to the top of the canopy to reach the sunlight. For this reason, I prefer to grow them along a sunny fence or up a trellis or sturdy arbor. Note that grapes are large vines and will develop heavy thick old-wood trunks, so any support you create for them will need to be study enough to bear the weight.

Fox grapes are North American native growing plants found along the East coast. Concord is a variety that many people will be familiar with and makes excellent jelly or juice. Most grape varieties are self-fruitful, although Muscadines sometimes require pollination from a male plant. Muscadines are also native to North America and were found in the Southwest, so you can see how they are more tolerant of the dry heat found there. We have them wild here in Oklahoma.

Training a grape up an arbor or along a fence takes some care and attention the few first years, but once the plants are well-established they are easy to maintain and do not require too much pampering. If you plant varieties particularly suited to your growing season you will have a lot more success with fewer headaches. Check with your local county extension office to get some ideas of what works well in your region.

To train your grapes, plant them near your support beams or poles and then train the strongest stem straight up the trellis to become the "trunk" of your grape vine. Allow side shoots to develop at regular intervals where fence beams are, or support beams on an arbor fall, but keep them trimmed to size so they don't grow too wide for the space. Each of these stems becomes a permanent branch across the top of the arbor or beam of the fence and is called a cordon. This process takes two years.

To maximize your fruit production, prune your grapes in late winter each year to keep the side branches trimmed back so fruiting occurs near the cordon and the vine doesn't overwhelm the arbor. Each year new fruit will be carried on the new shoots that grow from the cordon. You'll have lovely shade under your arbor, plus fruit for your table. Expect anywhere from 7–25 pounds of grapes beginning in year five, depending on the variety you grow.

POTENTIAL PESTS AND DISEASES

There are relatively few pests and diseases that attack grape vines as long as they are healthy and well suited for your region. Sometimes Japanese beetles are a problem and mildew can be a problem—especially in European varieties. Planting resistant varieties and providing good airflow through yearly pruning will help prevent mildew or rot. You will have to watch out for birds that enjoy your grapes as much as you do if you aren't careful!

HOW TO USE

With European and fox grapes, you'll harvest entire bunches of grapes when they are ripe, but cutting the stem above each plant keeps the grapes on their stems until you're ready to eat or use! Muscadines tend to ripen individually, however, so spread a sheet under the vine and give it a shake. Each day collect the ripe muscadines that drop, and leave the rest to further ripen.

Muscadines tend to have thicker skins and so are typically used for jellies and preserves, juice, or wine, making rather than fresh eating. All the other grapes have varieties that tend to be better for eating fresh, while others are recommended more as wine-making varieties, so do a little research before planting. Grapes are also delicious when dehydrated and made into raisins.

RECOMMENDATIONS

There are literally thousands of varieties of grapes, so I must preface this list by again recommending you consult a local winery in your area, or check with a county extension office in your area to determine what your region can grow. This firsthand knowledge will provide on-the-ground recognizance for you and save you a lot of heartbreak.

Because muscadine grows wild in our area, I know that the named varieties also do well. Black Fry is a female-only variety; however, the fruit is quite large and delicious. Carlos is self-pollinating, or perfect, and has blush-pink colored grapes. Jumbo has thinner-skinned grapes that can be eaten fresh and is another female-plant muscadine that needs a pollinator.

Among the fox grapes, Concord has a rich and familiar flavor. Reliance is a hybrid with better cold tolerance and gorgeous, rich red fruits. If you want white fox grapes, Edelweiss is lovely but doesn't do well in hot summer areas. Himrod is a hybrid that looks great on arbors because of its vigorous growth. I should also mention Fredonia, which ripens earlier than many other grapes.

If you wish to try the European grapes, pick up some of the more disease resistant and productive varieties. White Riesling does well in cooler climates and Black Monukka is one of the hardiest.

✿ Hops (*Humulus*)

Hops are one of those unique gems that has migrated from the agricultural world into the landscape community, and with good reason. Cast-off varieties that are unusually colored or too small for commercial use, have been adopted by home gardeners. Their loss is our gain!

BOTANICAL INFORMATION: *Deciduous Perennial*

Hops are hardy in zones 3–11 and these fast-growing vines will easily reach 15–25 feet in length. Use them to cover arbors and open patio screened roofs in the summer, for quick, seasonal shade just when you need it.

GROWING GUIDE

Hops need full sun and prefer well-draining, rich soil that can support their rapid growth rate. Typically, as long as they have full fun and the soil doesn't dry out, they will grow beautifully. Give them a trellis or vertical supports to climb and they will quickly cover it. They are less heavy than grapes, and the vines die back in winter so they can grow on a wider variety of supports than grapes.

The flower clusters hang from the stems in summer. Even though they aren't brightly colored, the form and movement is lovely. These become the cones from which hops are harvested for beer making. Harvesting is easy: simply pick the hops mid-August to early October when the outsides turn papery and become lighter in color. They have a pleasing, pine-like fragrance, so plant them where you can enjoy both the movement and scent in the wind. Typically each plant will produce about 1 pound of hops, give or take.

Note—The stems and leaves can be slightly irritating to the skin, especially in those with sensitive skin or allergies. I recommend wearing gloves when handling the vines and avoiding planting them over sitting areas where you might brush against them. Also of note is that only the female plants have the decorative (and useful) cones. If you grow hops from seeds you'll likely get half male and half female plants, while most nurseries will sell you rhizomes for the female plants.

Plant the rhizomes in early spring about 2 feet apart. You'll need to water semi-frequently the first year, and mulch to conserve water. Keep the feet of the hops weed-free to prevent competition, especially the first year when the plants are becoming established.

Summer Shandy hops by Proven Winner is just beginning to cover the vertical trellis. Photo courtesy of Proven Winners.

You may not see flowers the first year. In the winter, trim dead vines to ground level (be sure to add them to the compost bin). The new shoots will appear in the spring ready for action!

POTENTIAL PESTS AND DISEASES

Aphids and mites can sometimes invade hops, but a quick squirt with water will typically knock them lose. In some areas, powdery mildew can be a problem, so consider resistant strains or trim the leaves from the bottom few inches of the stems to allow more air circulation between the stems.

HOW TO USE

If you're a home brewer, you know how to use hops in that traditional method. However, hops have been used for medicinal purposes as well. The dried flowers can be brewed into a calming tea, which is said to help relieve anxiety. I find it adds a tart flavor and mix it with hibiscus and lemon grass.

One overlooked use of the hops vines, is the use of the shoots as asparagus-like food in the spring. Trim new shoots in the spring when they reach 12–18 inches. Not only will these thin stems grow easily up any trellis or support, but they are also a delicious and tender vegetable for spring dishes. Steam tender shoots or grill them for a tasty treat.

RECOMMENDATIONS

Willamette is a flavorful option that is also disease resistant against downy mildew. Summer Shandy is a newly released dwarf form by Proven Winners that has bright, golden foliage with vines about 10 feet long. Cascade is known for its citrus overtone and partial resistance to mildew. Golden Hops, one of the bitter varieties, has yellow toned foliage as well.

✿ Kiwi (*Actinidia* spp.)

Kiwifruit grows on deciduous vines and there are four main varieties that have varying zones of hardiness. You can expect to harvest 50–150 pounds of fruit per plant from these prolific vines except for Super-hardy kiwifruit, which produces about 10 pounds on average. All kiwifruit bear fruit on the female plants but need a male plant nearby to provide pollination.

Kiwi plants are both delicious and edible as well. Photo courtesy of Wendy Cutler.

BOTANICAL INFO: *Perennial Deciduous Vine*

- Kiwifruit (*Actinidia deliciosa*)- Hardy zones 7-9
- Golden kiwifruit (*Actinidia chinensis*)—Hardy zones 8-10
- Hardy kiwifruit (*Actinidia arguta*)—Hardy zones 4-9
- Super-hardy kiwifruit (*Actinidia kolomikta*)—Hardy zones 3-7

GROWING GUIDE

Plant kiwifruit as bare-root plants in the winter or early spring. They do not tolerate salinity well and want regular watering. Space them 15 feet apart and plant them in full-sun.

Only the variegated leaves of the male plant may want some light shade protection where temperatures get above 100 degrees.

Provide your kiwi vines with a sturdy support that can support them. The vines have strong, twisting stems that will develop woody stems with interesting peeling bark over time. This texture adds to their winter interest in the landscape. Prune old wood out every third or fourth year on a rotating basis so you are never trimming all the old shoots in one season. This will keep the plant in good vigor for many years.

Depending on the growth rate of your kiwifruit vines and your growing zone, you may need to prune the vine tips to inhibit growth. Some growths in the wild reportedly get up to 100 feet to reach the light above the canopies of the trees!

POTENTIAL PESTS AND DISEASES

Typically none! How awesome is that?

HOW TO USE

Begin harvesting the fuzzy-skinned varieties (*A. deliciousa* and *A. chinensis*) in the fall when the fruit begins to soften. They can ripen off the vine until the sweet kiwi flavor is ready. *A. deliciosa* is the type you typically see in the grocery stores, with large, sweet-yet-tangy fruit. Left too long on the vine and they may spoil or birds will eat them. Not all the fruit will ripen at the same time.

Hardy kiwifruit (*A. arguta*) have much smaller fruit, reaching only 1–2 inches in size, but they are typically sweeter. The fruit is hairless so it can be eaten skin and all. Super-hardy kiwi vines are typically grown for the showy, variegated foliage on the male plants, but the female vines will bear fruit earlier than your other kiwi varieties. Provide summer shade relief in the afternoons to keep the white tips of the leaves from burning. Harvest when the fruit begins to soften slightly, and the fruit tastes good. There are apparently super special sugar-measuring tests you can get to check your kiwifruit's ripeness level, but really—we are gardening like ninjas, not nerds. Who has time for that?

RECOMMENDATIONS

Among the fuzzy-skinned, more tropical kiwi choices, Saanichton was developed in Canada and has more cold-tolerance than other varieties. Vincent is a female, fruit-producing choice that needs the fewest cold chill hours and will perform the best in warm gardening zones if you're pushing the boundaries of the zone 10 range. Issai is a hardy kiwifruit (*A. arguta*) with perfect (self-pollinating) flowers, making it a great choice for smaller garden spaces where a male plant would take too much room. A hybrid hardy kiwi called Ken's Red grows a fruit with reddish flesh instead of the typical green. September Sun is a super-hardy cultivar where the female vines also display variegated foliage and is reported to have sweeter fruit.

Lingonberry flowers look similar to blueberry but grow only to ground cover size. Photo courtesy ofSue St Jean, founder of www.LessNoise-MoreGreen.com

✿ Lingonberry (*Vaccinium vitis-idaea*)

Lingonberries are related to blueberries and make beautiful, evergreen ground cover if you have the right climate.

BOTANICAL INFORMATION: *Evergreen Perennial*

Lingonberry is hardy in zones 4–7 and is a woody, shrubby ground cover that grows only a few inches tall, to 1 foot maximum height. It's an excellent foundation ground cover in full sun to part shade, depending on the strength of your summer heat.

GROWING GUIDE

Provide lingonberry with rich soil full of organic matter that is moist and acidic. It will do beautifully as a ground cover where blueberries and camellias thrive. Elemental sulfur is a good amendment that you can add to the soil to increase the acidity level as needed. Space your plants about 2 feet apart and they will slowly grow and fill in the gaps.

Lingonberries are sensitive to being transplanted, usually due to underwatering in the first year. Keep the ground watered well enough to support the plants until their shallow root system can become better established. Mulch plants well to smother out weeds that will compete them out or take the water they need the first year. These are definitely not the ground covers you want in a drought area.

Healthy leaves are bright, glossy green and make an excellent foil to show off flowering shrubs in your garden. In the spring, the new foliage growth can be red-tinged. Sometimes the fall foliage will turn orange or reddish color. It's underused in the landscape in my opinion. It doesn't do well in my area's blistering triple-digit summers, but if you have cooler summers definitely try this ground cover.

POTENTIAL PESTS AND DISEASES

The biggest problem lingonberry faces is competition from weeds, so be sure to remove any weeds before planting and then mulch well.

HOW TO USE

Lingonberries can be used in any recipe that you'd use cranberries, but you can decrease the sugar ratio. They are just enough sweeter than cranberries to tolerate eating fresh if you pick them when perfectly ripe. They store well in the fridge and will keep for a few weeks! They are heavily used in Scandinavian dishes in everything from meat mixes to alcohol flavoring.

RECOMMENDATIONS

There is a surprising number of named cultivars available, considering how rarely home gardeners use lingonberries in the landscape; however, some are developed in Europe and may be difficult to find in the States. Red Pearl is readily available and is a more upright choice reaching over a foot tall. Dwarf or Minus reaches only 6 inches tall and has pink flowers with pea-size fruit but does best when interplanted with another cultivar for better pollination. Balsgard is a heavy producer growing 8 inches tall, and also needs another cultivar for best production. Ida is one of my favorite choices because it's a great size at 8 inches tall and is a reblooming variety that will produce two crops each year. Erntesegen is a German award-winning variety that has larger leaves.

✿ Malabar Spinach (*Basella alba*)

While it's not botanically related to spinach, the attractive heart-shaped leaves resemble spinach and the taste is reminiscent of spinach. The texture is a bit different, but the uses in kitchen are similar. It is, however, totally different in the landscape.

BOTANICAL INFORMATION: *Herbaceous Perennial Vine*

Hardy in zones 9–11, Malabar spinach is easily grown as an annual in other areas and will tolerate a tremendous amount of summer heat.

GROWING GUIDE

Malabar spinach is actually a perennial vine with attractive leaves. It would be excellent as a landscape ornamental, even if the leaves weren't a useful edible! The vines thrive in summer's heat, quickly reaching 6 feet in length. It's perfect for a summer shade on a patio or privacy screening for outdoor parties during the entertaining season. The leaves are a bright glossy green, while the stems are more burgundy colored, creating a lovely contrast.

Start Malabar spinach outdoors when the evening temperatures reach 55 degrees or higher. You can start indoors if your growing season is shorter to give them a jump-start. The seeds might take awhile to germinate, so don't despair; they are slow starters. Scarify the seeds (a fancy way of saying scrape the outer coating with sandpaper or on rough concrete to scrape it up a little) for better germination rates. Two weeks later, you should begin to see shoots. They will grow slowly as long as temps are still mild. As soon as you start thinking, "What a joke! This author doesn't know what she's talking about," summer will warm up and they will take off. I promise.

Malabar spinach vines aren't too heavy so they can be grown up a light trellis or chain-link fence. Anywhere pea vines grow in the cool seasons, malabar spinach will grow in the warm season, so they make good companions in the same planter. As soon as the soil reaches temperatures in the 80s, your pea vines will quit and your malabar will shoot up.

The vines will naturally die back with first frosts. You can take clippings from the growing tips prior to first frost and start the clippings indoors for replanting the following season, or simply replant seeds next year. They won't overwinter beyond zones 9 or possibly 8 with winter mulching and protection.

POTENTIAL PESTS AND DISEASES

Pest free. If the plant dries out too much, the leaves can become more bitter in flavor.

HOW TO USE

Harvest the tender leaves any time throughout the season. Don't harvest all the leaves from a single vine; there will be plenty for you to use by collecting a few leaves from each vine. The texture is different than spinach, so taste a few leaves to see whether you want them as a stand-alone salad ingredient or mixed with other greens and ingredients. They can also be boiled and used in omelets, sliced and added to stir-fry, and toss into soups or stews for added nutrition. I prefer it cooked over raw, but everyone has a difference preference.

RECOMMENDATIONS

There is a native variety that has green stems; however, most nurseries offer the red-stemmed variety. It's very attractive, so I recommend getting the red-stemmed variety for the added interest.

✿ Maypop—see Passion Fruit in this chapter

✿ Melon (*Cucurbitaceae Family*)

While melons, like cantaloupes and watermelon, are usually thought of as fruit, they are botanically vegetables in the gourd family. I don't care where the scientists place them; I love the sweet, juicy melons. And I definitely put them in a fruit salad, not a veggie salad.

Photo courtesy of M. Williams, founder of A Moveable Garden.

BOTANICAL INFORMATION: *Warm-Season Annual Vine*

- Melons (*Cucumis melo*)
- Muskmelons (the group where cantaloupes belong) (*C. m. reticulatus*)
- Late melons (these include honeydew and casaba melons) (*C. m. inodorus*)
- Watermelon (*Citrullus lanatus*)

These vining plants are annuals and produce sweet fruit in as little as 60 days, although some varieties take twice that or more.

GROWING GUIDE

Plant seeds directly outdoors after the last-frost date because these warm-season plants are sensitive to winter temperatures. Germination will be best when you have temperatures over 50 degrees at night. I tend to put more than one seed in each hole, and space each planting about 1 foot apart. I can always thin the seedlings if all the seeds come up but I hate bare spots in the garden, especially in an edible landscape design where the garden is "on display.

Most melons grow naturally on vines, which sometimes reach up to 6 feet. Their lovely, broader leaves are heavily lobed and attractive, and intersperse well with ornamentals. They can actually make a lovely, rambling ground cover in a sunny bed or border, where flowering herbs and shrubs are planted in the background. Smaller-fruiting varieties will stay light enough to grow vertically on a trellis support. Consider also growing small varieties from above with a large hanging basket, raised bed planter, container, or even on a sloping hillside that is difficult to keep in grass. The draping vines will reward you with a lovely cascading effect all summer, with delicious melons to harvest as a bonus.

Melons need sun. And lots of it. If you're in a short-summer area, plant them near a wall or solid fence where the sun's rays will be reflected back onto the plants. If your season is short, start them indoors during the winter and then transplant when temperatures warm up in the spring. I use biodegradable pots because in my experience some types of melons don't transplant well when their roots are disturbed.

Each kind of melon is unique for telling when it's ready to harvest—some turn a different color, some slip easily off the vine, some make a unique sound when thumped. The best bet is to check the growing instructions for specific melons or talk to a neighbor who has grown them for first-hand experience. Most quality nurseries and seed sellers are happy to talk through this with you as well, when you place your order. (See http://UntrainedHousewife.com/EdibleLandscapingResources for always up-to-date recommendations of companies I know and trust.)

Some books recommend using black plastic to heat up the soil and to protect the melon from lying directly on the ground. I prefer to avoid plastic in the garden for ecological reasons. I use cardboard if I want to protect a melon from wet soil. However, our climate is usually not dangerously moist for melons and a simple layer of mulch is sufficient.

POTENTIAL PESTS AND DISEASES

Melons can be attacked by cucumber beetles—real pests that not only destroy the vines but also spread diseases like mildew or leaf spot from plant to plant as well. Little blood suckers! Okay, sap suckers, but still—evil creatures. A pyrethrum spray when you see the first hint of beetles will help keep them under control. Don't wait too long; use it as soon as you notice the beetles and it will be easier to get them under control.

HOW TO USE

Once you harvest your melons, just eat! Most can be eaten fresh or used in a variety of light, summer dessert recipes. With most melons, you cut the fruit open, scoop out the seeds and stringy pulp, and then eat the colorful flesh off the rind. Watermelon rind is used in some preserving recipes but does not compare to the joy of eating fresh, fridge-cold melon on a hot summer day. Mmmmmm …

RECOMMENDATIONS

For the purposes of edible landscaping, get vines that produce smaller fruit or attractive ornamental fruits. There are hundreds of options out there, so I'm only highlighting a few suitable for trellises, containers, and arbors. Cucumber melon is sometimes called vine peach because of its small size. It is *C. m.* var. *chito* melon scientifically. The vines grow to 10 feet, a perfect length for archway or arbor in the summer. Rich Sweetness is a Russian melon described to me by Baker Creek Seeds as reddish-orange with yellow tiger stripes, which sounds like something I simply must try in my garden soon. Minnesota Midget is well suited, as you might guess by the name, to shorter season areas; it is ready to harvest in only 65 days. It has a compact, 3-inch vine as well, perfect for a trailing effect over a raised bed or container. New Orchid is a hybrid watermelon that produces small, 7-pound fruit with a deep green rind color. Sugar Baby has such a dark green color that it's almost black, with bright red flesh, and grows 8 pounds in size.

✿ Mint, creeping forms—*see growing information in Chapter 7*

✿ Nasturtium (*Tropaeolum* spp.)

These lovely plants used to be grown in the vegetable gardens of early settlers, leading to their acceptance as a cottage garden plant. They are equally at home in an ornamental planting and in the vegetable garden. They are both gorgeous and quite tasty.

Photo courtesy of Alfred Diem.

BOTANICAL INFO: *Annual*

Grown in full sun to part shade, nasturtiums are typically grown as climbing or cascading plants. Two species are hybrids and are used in the landscape and kitchen, *T. majus* and *T. minus*. There are other Tropaeolum plants grown for their edible tubers, but these are by far the loveliest landscaping plants.

GROWING GUIDE

Sow nasturtium seeds directly in the garden where you want these charmers to grow, and they will readily germinate in mid-spring and begin flowering a few weeks after that. In zones 9–11 they will readily self-sow themselves and can even be considered slightly invasive. If they are invasive where you live, plant them in containers or contained borders.

Their rounded, saucer-shaped leaves are so unique and always remind me of lily pads. The broad rounded form contrasts beautifully with all the other plants in the garden. And then there are the flowers—wow! Lots of color options to choose from.

Nasturtiums come in solid colors or have multi-colored blooms with colored eyes in a range of colors: red, orange, yellow, peach, cream, and almost any combination of these colors.

Climbing nasturtiums can reach up to 10 feet long and make excellent companions for scarlet runners, malabar spinach, or tomatoes on a trellis or obelisk planting. Or let the vines ramble along the ground hiding leggy stems of woody herbs, peppers, or other edibles in the landscape. You really can't go wrong with these as long as they have part sun or better.

Soil too rich in nitrogen can cause leggy vines with lush leaf growth and very few flowers. These edibles do better with poor soil, so I like to rotate them in spaces after heavier feeders like broccoli or tomatoes. They are moderately drought-tolerant so they do well in containers and raised beds where their cascading nature is most attractive.

POTENTIAL PESTS AND DISEASES

Nasturtiums are sometimes planted as "trap crops" around monoculture fields. This means they attract pests like cucumber beetles and aphids that would otherwise attack other plants. The bugs swarm a nasturtium plant instead of the more expensive crop, and the nasturtium can be dug up and burned off without having to spray the crop. You may find aphids or beetles doing this in your garden, so attracting beneficial insects with a diverse landscape plan will be important if you find this to be the case. Insecticidal soap spray is an organic way to treat for aphids and mites as well.

HOW TO USE

All parts of the nasturtium are edible—flowers, leaves, shoots, and seeds. The nasturtium has a crisp, mustard-like flavor and was compared to cress in early writings. Use the leaves to replace lettuce in a sandwich, use the seeds to flavor vinegar for unique dressings and stir fry, or just pick the flowers to include in your summer salads. They are easy to use and add a lot of zest and body to many summer dishes.

RECOMMENDATIONS

Alaska Series nasturtiums have really pretty light green and white variegated foliage that adds a bright, eye-catching pop as a ground cover. My favorite in this series is Alaska Red, which has a deep red flower I just adore. Moonlight is a rare heirloom variety with pale yellow flowers and 6 foot long vines. Vesuvius is an unusual pastel coral bloom—a really pretty salmon color. This is a shorter bush form that grows a foot tall and wide. Jewel Mix is another dwarf form with bright colors in a mix of yellows, oranges, and reds. Milkmaid is a pale cream color, the closest to white of any nasturtium, and grows on compact vines. Tall Trailing nasturtium is a mix of yellow, orange, and golden flowers with long vines reaching up to 10 feet in length.

Photo courtesy of M. Williams, founder of A Moveable Garden.

☆ Passion Fruit (*Passiflora* spp.)

A native vine of North America it is found wild in many areas of the Southeast in fencerows, woodland edges, or open areas of the forests.

BOTANICAL INFO: *Herbaceous Perennial Vine*

Passiflora incarnata and *Passiflora caerulea* produce edible fruits. They are found natively to zones 8 or 7, but with winter protection can survive as far as zone 5.

GROWING GUIDE

These robust vines produce a unique and beautiful flower called the passion flower, which will later produce an apple-sized fruit, often called maypops. They appear rather late in the spring, about the time hostas start making their appearance. But once the vines begin growing, they grow fast and will be blooming only 4–5 weeks later. Soil should be well draining, but moist, although established plants will tolerate some periods of lower watering. Because of these preferences, this plant does well in container plantings.

The gorgeous flower is what has kept passion fruit vines so popular as an ornamental. The flowers are usually deep purple and white, with structural centers that make them truly eye-catching. The flowers are also highly fragrant, making them a nice choice for a sunny patio or arbor where you will spend time on a summer afternoon.

The leaves are a lovely glossy green on vigorous vines that grow 10 feet or longer, depending on your climate. Let the vines climb over a trellis, fence, or even spring-flowering shrub that blooms in early spring.

Maypops spread via runners underground, so you may need to pull volunteer sprouts in future years. For this reason, the vines are sometimes considered invasive, but it seems a small price to pay for the beauty and delicious fruit. Not every flower on the plant is a perfect flower. If you want the best fruiting possible, hand-pollination will be helpful.

POTENTIAL PESTS AND DISEASES

Maypops need very little maintenance and care, and do not have many pest or disease problems.

HOW TO USE

Maypop fruit ripens on the vine over a prolonged period of time. The skin may become slightly wrinkled, or begin to turn yellow, when the fruit is ripe. Maypops will easily break open with pressure when they are ripe, revealing the dark seeds and pulp inside. Like pomegranates, you can pop the pulp into your mouth, suck the juice, and spit out the seed, or eat it seed and all depending on your preference.

Maypop has to be handled carefully or the ripe fruit could break. It may pop open, hence the common name. This is also one reason why it's not grown commercially because shipping cross-country would be a nightmare. Thankfully your ninja gardening skills solves that problem entirely, and you can enjoy this fruit fresh from your own yard.

The vines and leaves were historically dried and used as a sedative herb. The tea was thought to counteract anxiety, nervousness, and sleep disorders. Dehydrating is the best way to preserve the plant, while jams or jelly is the best way to preserve the fruit.

RECOMMENDATIONS

While the official varieties are gorgeous in and of themselves, there are named cultivars sometime available as well. Any maypop will be a rock star in the garden, but here are some you might want to look for. 'Blue' has a pale blue or lavender color compared to the native *P. incarnata*, and is sometimes sold simply as *P. caerulea*. Lady Margaret is a hybrid with ruby-rose flowers and white centers that really stand out against the green lobed leaves. Alba is, as you might expect, a white flowering hybrid and has very fragrant blooms.

☆ Pea (*Pisum sativum*)

These cold-season plants are a classic cottage garden addition. They ramble along fences, arbors, or garden archways.

BOTANICAL INFO: ANNUAL *Cool-Season Vine*

Pea vines are cool-season plants that will shut down all production once the temperature warms up too much. There are actually five types of peas:

- Snow peas (*P.S. var macrocarpon*)
- Snap peas (*P.S. var macrocarpon*)
- Shelling peas
- Soup peas
- Shoots and leaves peas (*Usui*)

What's in a name?

Here's a sneaky ninja-trick for you when you are shopping at garden centers and in catalogs, trying to find the right plant. When the label says "alba," the plant will have white flowers. When the label says "variegata," the leaves will be variegated.

GROWING GUIDE

Peas really thrive best in areas with long, cool springs. That is, not where I live. We get better success growing them in the fall because of our typically slow decline into the winter season. Either way, spring or fall, peas prefer those mild temperatures and provide colorful flowers, and lush vines, in a season when not many other plants are thriving.

Plant peas extremely early in spring or in the fall as a cool-season crop. Seeds are large and easy to handle. Plant them about ¾-inch deep and provide well-watered, but not soggy, soil. Watch out! Mice like to eat newly planted pea seeds before they have a chance to germinate. You want the temperature to be below 75 degrees in the fall before planting your fall garden crop.

Soaking peas overnight will help your germination rates. Inoculate your seeds prior to planting to activate their nitrogen-fixing capabilities unless you've grown peas in the area before. Water the ground well prior to planting so you can hold off watering until the shoots have appeared to prevent rotting.

Give peas full sun unless you're in a hot-summer area where afternoon shade may extend your growing season by a week or two. Mulch will help keep peas evenly watered unless slugs are a big problem in your area.

All peas, even the so-called bush forms, benefit from trellising or support of some kind. Even the bush types are really just short vines, and will have less disease if you give them support. The tendrils on the pea vines will easily clasp and climb any support given with little training required on your part.

Snow peas are harvested while the pea pods are still flat. Photo courtesy of Liz West.

The tendrils on the pea vines will easily clasp and climb any support given with little training required on your part. Alternatively, plant one of the dwarf 2–3 foot varieties as an edge on a raised bed or container planting and let the tendrils grow down the side of the container. Once they are started, there's nothing more you need to do but enjoy the gorgeous flowers and wait for the fruit to appear!

The legume flowers are attractively colored, even in the most boring of pea varieties. The shoots themselves are edible, so if you thin extra pea shoots, cook them up with a stir-fry and don't let them go to waste! When the flowers begin to set pods, watch your vines carefully. Harvest pea pods sooner than later because once the seeds mature, the vine will stop producing.

Snow peas are picked at about 2–3 inches long while the pods are still flat. Snap peas are left until the pods begin to swell and fill out. Shelling peas are left even longer until the seeds inside have fully grown and the pods are almost totally round. Like corn, the sugars decrease the second they are picked, so enjoy the peas fresh for the sweetest taste.

In the landscape I love to pair pea vines with something that does best in summer weather, and plant them both in the same place. For example pea vines and malabar spinach (also described in this chapter) would be a perfect combination. Just as peas are giving up for the season in late spring, or early summer, the malabar spinach will begin to take off. Conversely, planting peas in late summer means that by the time malabar is finished for the fall, the pea vine will be well-established and begin it's winter flowering. One space, multiple seasons of beauty and productivity. Talk about gardening like a ninja!

POTENTIAL PESTS AND DISEASES

Unfortunately, peas can be prone to several pests and diseases. Powdery mildew will occur when there isn't good air circulation and aphids are often a challenge. Peas also attract ladybug larvae. Before you spray with insecticidal soap, check your plants for beneficial insects first. Your local county extension office will know what diseases and pests are most common in your area so you can plant peas that are more resistant to the problems in your specific area.

HOW TO USE

Snap and snow peas can be eaten whole-pod. They are great in stir-fry dishes or sautéed, of course. But sweet tender pods picked short enough to be bite-sized can be added whole to early spring salads for a crunchy, sweet addition. Shelling peas are popped open and the round sweet peas removed. Peas can be dried for long-term storage, eaten as sweet peas, or blended into delicious soups. Peas are very versatile and used in a wide variety of ways in the kitchen.

RECOMMENDATIONS

Alaska is an early maturing soup pea perfect for areas with short growing seasons. Alderman or Telephone Tall fusarium are resistant heirloom shelling pea. Wando is an heirloom with both cold and heat tolerance. Sugar Sprint is a snap pea with lots of disease resistance that also matures within 65 days and only grows about 2 feet tall. Blue Pod Capucijners is a soup pea with deep purple flowers and pods. Golden Sweet is a gorgeous pale-yellow podded snow pea that will stand out with it's unique coloring.

✿ Squash, summer and winter (*Curcurbita* spp.)

All squashes are warm-season growers with similar growing requirements. The difference between summer squash and winter squash has more to do with when they are harvested than their growing conditions, so I'll talk about them all here. Note that while bush forms exist, the vines are the best for edible landscape situations. Their broad-leafed rambling vines will be the focus of my growing guide and plant recommendations here. See Chapter 7 for some recommendations of a few select bush forms.

BOTANICAL INFORMATION: *Annual Warm-Season Vine*

- *Curcurbita maxima*—Many winter squashes and pumpkins are *C. maxima*.
- *Curcurbita moschata*—Many butternuts and Italian heirloom squashes fall into this variety classification.
- *Curcurbita pepo*—Most summer squashes and zucchini are *C. pepo*.
- *Curcurbita mixta*
- *Cucumis sativus*—Cucumbers

These classifications are by no means set in stone. I've found that the scientific classification is less important that the summer versus winter squash classification. Cucumbers are in the same family as squash and are grown like summer squashes, so I'm including their growing information here.

GROWING GUIDE

Squash seeds should be planted in rich soil that has been well amended with plenty of compost as they are heavy feeders. Summer squash are usually harvested early while the fruit is smaller, and so typically need less nitrogen than their greedier, winter squash brothers. Seeds are planted relatively deep—up to an inch deep—in warm, spring soil after the last frost.

Space your seeds a foot apart if you plan to grow them vertically, or 6 feet apart if you plan to let them grow horizontally. Yes, 6 feet—that's pretty intensive planting since many can reach 15 feet or more in length. Amazing, isn't it?

Squash vines can easily clamber up any support within their grasp.

Mulch your squash seedlings well to help keep moisture in the soil. The vines require a moderate amount of water to support themselves, so these aren't the ground covers I would choose for a xeriscape, or drought-tolerant garden area. Once your vines reach a good length, they will quickly begin to flower. Male flowers appear before the female flowers; sometimes hand-pollination is needed to help ensure good fruiting. If you've planted lots of pollinator attracting plants in the area (see Hell-Strip Design, pp. 57–61), that will also help ensure good fruit production.

Once the female bloom is pollinated, the tiny fruit bump at the end of the blossom begins to swell and grows into the squash you are hoping for. While zucchini is probably the squash you're most familiar with, squash comes in a huge variety of colors and sizes and shapes. Choose a variety of heirloom and hybrid options for the pops of color they can provide!

I love using squash as a weed-smothering ground cover in a sunny perennial bed because the vines will quickly fill in a new planter while your perennials are still getting established. Some gardeners still use the Three-Sisters method of planting: squash vines as a lush ground cover through corn fields. Another great use of squash is up an arbor or trellis. I've also seen pathways covered with temporary archways and squash vines grown up both sides. This provides lovely shaded walkways through a garden area in the summer when it's needed and also delicious edibles at the same time!

Don't let the vines dry out or wilt. In areas like mine, this means a good layer of mulch and planting the squash where watering will be easier to do. Summer squash are ready to harvest as soon as 40–60 days, while winter squash will be harvested much later. Check the growing information for each type you want to make sure you'll have enough frost-free days!

Summer squash are harvested early. They are called summer squash because they are picked when the fruit is young and the skins thin, making them unsuitable for long-term storage. Harvest the ready fruit daily, or every other day at the least, because any seeds that mature will cause the vine to stop producing new flowers and fruit. Harvesting regularly helps the vines stay more productive.

Winter squash, on the other hand, is left on the vine much longer and develops a thick, strong skin. This thick skin makes them much better suited for long-term storage, which means you can eat fresh, homegrown produce all winter long! Winter squash can tolerate a light touch of frost and colder days at the end of its growing cycle. But a hard frost will hurt the ability to be stored long-term.

POTENTIAL PESTS AND DISEASES

I'm sure it will come as no shock that the worst pests you'll face are squash beetles. We gardeners are a creative bunch when it comes to naming the pests, I tell ya. Squash beetles should have been named horror bugs because they are gruesome looking pests that are hard to kill. You can cover the squash with floating row covers to prevent egg laying. If you do this for too long, you'll need to hand pollinate your squash since the bees won't be able to get in either.

Every good ninja warrior needs a sidekick, so we also use our chickens for some natural pest control. If you aren't able to have chickens, you can handpick the squash beetle adults once they first appear, but warning—those monstrous devils can fly. Water your squash vines first, and they won't be able to fly as well so you can catch them easier. When I find a cluster of the orangey-brown eggs on the underside of a squash leaf, I take great delight in smearing them into oblivion.

Just to keep things interesting, other pests include aphids, cucumber beetles (cucumbers are closely related to squashes), mites, and squash vine borers. The latter are particularly insidious because they chew a hole into the vine near the ground level and then chew their way up the vine to eat the fruit. They are most attracted to pumpkins, it seems, and I've had some small luck saving the runners if I catch the borers quickly enough. If you see the entrance hole, you can dig the borer out of the vine without destroying all the vessels in the runner. Just slice

Cucumber takes center stage as it climbs the simple trellis in this mixed container. Photo first appeared in *Easy Container Combos: Vegetables & Flowers* and is used courtesy of Pamela Crawford.

the vine vertically—just making a slit with a sharp knife. It isn't easy—you may cut up the vine stalk until you find the borer and dig it out.

The most important method of controlling pests in the home garden is to rotate crops and dispose of the leftovers. Parasitic nematodes can also be an important method of organic control. We compost all the vines each year so any bugs trying to overwinter in the debris are destroyed. I also plant the squash vines alternating years with beans (see earlier in this chapter). This not only foils pests from developing a stronghold, but also helps replenish nitrogen after growing the heavy-feeding squash.

HOW TO USE

There are so many uses for squash! It starts with their edible flowers, which can be eaten right off the vine, fried, or sautéed. Summer squash is often eaten raw and fresh in a variety of dishes. Slices of cucumbers or zucchini can be used as a meat replacement in sandwiches, used to infuse water with flavor and nutrients, eaten in a variety of salads, salsas, and casseroles, and so on.

We also pickle many summer squashes to preserve them for eating later, and freeze quite a few for use in winter stews. Add them into any slow-cooker stew an hour before serving (longer than that breaks them down too much in my opinion), and you'll have a little taste of summer in your bowl in December.

Winter squash is often cooked in pies, casseroles, soups, and sauces. Chunk it up and roast it or make a yummy puree. I don't like it mushy—a short roast in the oven with some butter and sea salt is a yummy treat for me. The large, mature seeds of winter squash is also a treat when roasted in the oven with salt or other seasonings. Pumpkin seeds are especially well-known for their nutritive and delicious value.

RECOMMENDATIONS

It's hard to go wrong with any of the squashes and gourds available, but I'll highlight some of my favorites for use in a home garden design.

Cucumbers: Lemon Cuke is a cute, rounded yellow cucumber that is mild tasting and looks great in the garden. White Wonder is a white-fruited variety and stands out because of the unique coloring. Satsuki Midori is more beetle resistant and tolerates some shade as well.

Summer Squashes: Black Beauty is a classic zucchini with very dark green skin. Tromboncino, or Zucchetta rampicante, is an Italian heirloom that grows prolifically and is resistant to squash borer. The fruits will grow long but taste better when harvested under 9 inches. Golden Dawn and Golden Zucchini are both upright bush form plants that produce pretty yellow fruits. Delicata is an heirloom squash with unusual white fruit with green ribs creating a pretty striped effect. It climbs happily up a trellis or fence and can be harvested as a summer squash or left to ripen as a winter squash.

Winter Squashes: Amazonka is a short-vined heirloom variety that grows only 4 foot long with small, orange pumpkins that reach about 3 pounds in size. It's perfect for edging large containers, draping over raised walls, or in smaller spaces. Red Kuri is a gorgeous variety that produces deep red-orange fruit that reaching 5–10 pounds in size. White Wonder is a white vining pumpkin and White Acorn is a bush form plant, but both produce moderate-sized white fruit that stands out against the green leaves. Scarlet is an acorn or butternut-type squash with attractive bright red-orange color and great taste.

Photo courtesy of Alexis Watters, founder of BeanAndBee.com

✿ Strawberry (*Fragaria* spp.)

Long a part of cottage gardens and kitchen gardens, the strawberry plant may seem relatively small, but it produces some of the most popular soft fruit you can grow.

BOTANICAL INFORMATION: *Short-Lived Perennial*

- Garden Strawberry (*Fragaria ananassa*)—Comes in three categories: Day-neutral, spring-bearing, and ever-bearing.
- Alpine Strawberry (*Fragaria vesca* or sometimes *Fragaria alpina*)

GROWING GUIDE

Strawberries are unsung heroes of the edible landscape. They are beautiful, clumping herbaceous plants that stay small enough to be easily contained, have charming apple-like blooms, and of course, produce delicious fruit. Plant strawberry crowns or roots in the late fall where winters are mild. In cooler climates, plant in early spring as soon as you can work the soil.

Strawberries tolerate cold weather well but will stop producing flowers and fruit when the weather gets above 90 degrees. Therefore, all varieties, especially Alpines, will appreciate a little bit of evening shade in hotter climates. A good layer of mulch over the garden soil is always appreciated as well. Keep the soil consistently moist and water at ground level to help prevent spreading diseases.

Strawberries don't need nitrogen-rich fertilizers if you want plenty of fruit, but will benefit from growing in soil that is well amended with plenty of organic matter. For spring-bearing and ever-bearing strawberries, you can remove the flowers the first year to allow better root development. You'll end up with more berries the following year. Although I must be honest, I usually forget to do this. I've started planting Alpine berries so I can stop fussing with this type of "pruning" altogether.

I love to use strawberries as border or edging plants. They mix well interplanted between larger perennials and shrubs as a ground cover as well. I've also seen some amazing hanging baskets with strawberries, but in our area they dry out too quickly to be practical. Day-neutral and Alpines will provide a longer-lasting harvest over several weeks in the spring and summer versus a single flush of berries. The garden berries typically need full sun for best berry production, while Alpines tolerate shade much better.

Alpines are clumping strawberries that do not send out runners, but some strawberries do. If your strawberries send out runners, let the new plants at the end begin to take root, and then cut the runner to create a brand-new plant. Strawberries tend to die out after a few years, so these new plants will keep a bed renewed. Sometimes digging the main strawberry plant and dividing it will help renew waning strawberries.

POTENTIAL PESTS AND DISEASES

Probably one of the biggest problems with strawberries is root rot. Be sure not to plant your crowns too deep or to keep the soil too soggy. Leaf diseases like mildew, leaf spot, or leaf blight can be tough. And, of course, slugs, aphids, mites and other pests will appreciate a juicy strawberry plant. Keeping your plants healthy, removing rotting fruit quickly, and using natural pest control for slugs will help get a good crop from your edible beds and borders.

HOW TO USE

Strawberries are used often to flavor many dishes and desserts. In addition to using them fresh, berries can be frozen or dehydrated for long-term storage. The berries are very nutritious and high in many micronutrients and vitamins.

Not only are the fruit delicious, of course, but the leaves make a soothing tea rich in both vitamin C and iron. Brew a tea with the fresh leaves, or dry the leaves for storage for tea later.

RECOMMENDATIONS

Alpine: Try White Delight or Yellow Yonder for fruit that isn't the typical red, which helps to foil birds from eating your fruit before you can. I love the red berries, though. For northern friends, Improved Rugan is cold tolerant to zone 3. Attila is a unique alpine that sends runners and makes a dramatic container planting. You really can't do wrong with any of the alpine strawberries because even though the fruit is smaller, it is more flavorful than regular strawberries.

Garden Strawberry: Alice is an early fruiting variety with an extended growing season. Toscana is a gorgeous ever-bearing hybrid that has hot pink flowers and beautiful trailing runners. Seascape is a day-neutral berry that does best north of zone 8. Tristar is day-neutral and has excellent hardiness no matter where you live (heat tolerance included). Quinalt is an ever-bearing strawberry that produces fruit very quickly and will do well in a hanging basket or less-permanent container.

✿ Sweet Potato (*Ipomea batatas*)

BOTANICAL INFO: *Perennial Vining Root Crop*

This warm-season crop is actually related to morning glory vines, which you'll see when you observe how beautiful the plant's flowers are. Even though sweet potatoes are botanically a perennial, they are grown as an annual because the edible roots are harvested for eating

GROWING GUIDE

Shoots, called slips, are planted to start the sweet potatoes each year. These shoots have been cultivated from the tubers in the previous year. Plant your slips in soil that has plenty of organic matter mixed into it. While sweet potatoes can tolerate and produce in poor soil, the vines will be longer (and thus the root crop better) with compost and good soil. Just don't feel like you have to over-fertilize with nitrogen-rich fertilizers or you'll have vines for days and fewer roots.

Sweet potatoes typically need a good deal of sunny, frost-free days for a good crop, which is why they are thought of as southern plants. Earlier maturing or more cold-tolerant varieties can be grown further north, however, so careful selection for your region is the key to success. Plant these beautiful plants in containers, raised beds, or even mixed with perennials as an attractive ground cover.

Traditionally, sweet potatoes are grown in raised hills because they need great drainage to prevent rot, which makes them perfect for a large container. Use light soil that isn't too heavy or filled with clay or the tubers will be too small. If your soil is compact, you'll want to till and add bulky amendments, or grow in a container where you can add a good soil mix.

Harvest when the tops begin to die back, when the mature date is reached (usually around 115 days or so), or when danger of first frost presents itself. Once you've dug your sweet potatoes, they need to be cured for better storage ability. Spread them out on newspaper in a dark, dry room in a single layer. Let the skin harden and dry for the next 7–10 days. Then brush off any loose dirt and they will store well for weeks. The curing process also sweetens the potato so don't skip it, even if you plan to eat them all as quickly as possible!

POTENTIAL PESTS AND DISEASES

Potatoes can build up diseases in the soil if they are grown in the same ground year after year. If you use containers for your sweet potatoes, consider freshening the soil each year. Otherwise, rotate sweet potatoes with another crop—they swap well with squash plants in the garden as they are both warm-season plants. Watch out for pests that attack the vines such as aphids or flea beetles.

Even this edible sweet potato has beautiful flowers and ornamental vining foliage. Photo courtesy of Alicia Z, founder of WalkingSoftlyUponTheEarth.com.

HOW TO USE

Sweet potatoes can be baked, roasted, pureed, mashed, and so on. They are even made into pies and breads. Their sweet flavor and high nutrition value make them a welcome addition to many meals. Once cured, they will store in a cool, dry, dark place for several weeks with no loss of quality and continue to provide food well into the winter months.

RECOMMENDATIONS

In addition to the historic orange-fleshed sweet potatoes, there are several uniquely colored options when you delve into the heirloom selections as well. Beauregard is a burgundy vine potato with sweet orange flesh that does well in cooler climate zones. Vardaman is more compact and does well in smaller spaces. Nancy Hall has yellow flesh and is resistant to rot. Molokai Purple is a rare purple-fleshed type that is very high in antioxidants. Jersey Yellow is a firm potato with creamy, light-yellow flesh.

✿ Sweet Woodruff (*Galium odoratum*)

A sweetly fragrant, semi-evergreen ground cover that grows in part shade and is hardy zones 4–8.

BOTANICAL INFORMATION: *Semi-Evergreen Perennial Ground Cover*

A highly fragrant ground cover that performs well with fragrant flowers in moist shade gardens.

GROWING GUIDE

Sweet Woodruff is a native woodland ground cover that grows between 6–12 inches tall. Its woodland history explains the inspiration for how I used the plant in this garden design. It naturalizes well and will spread to fill in under the shrubs and trees in this garden design with little effort.

In fact, I recommend keeping it limited to enclosed borders like this one, containers, or raised beds, to prevent it from invading more of your garden area than you intend. In mild winter areas, it is nearly evergreen but will not tolerate too-humid summers, which limits it's southern range.

Sweet woodruff is a lovely shade ground cover with a pleasing fragrance as well. Photo courtesy of Patrick Standish.

POTENTIAL PESTS AND DISEASES

Very few pests and diseases.

HOW TO USE

Traditionally used with strawberries to flavor May wine, there's mixed warnings on other internal uses beyond the use of alcohol flavoring. I like to dehydrate it for use in potpourri sachets and recently discovered that it can be used as a natural dye source.

RECOMMENDATIONS

I haven't found any named varieties listed for this herb.

✿ Thyme (*Thymus* spp.)

One of my favorite herbs for the edible landscape or any landscape actually.

BOTANICAL INFO: *Semi-Evergreen Perennial Herb*

Thyme is hardy in zones 5–9 and is consistently evergreen in my zone 7 garden. With protection, it will probably survive through zone 4 as well.

- Common Thyme—*Thymus vulgaris*
- Lemon Thyme—*Thymus citriodorus*
- Caraway Thyme—*Thymus herba-barona*
- Wild Thyme—*Thymus pulegiodes*
- Creeping Thyme—*Thymus praecox*

GROWING GUIDE

Thyme is so easy to grow. I love using it in visible areas that are further out and won't be tended as frequently, like mailbox planters or driveway edges. (See Hell-Strip Design, pp. 57–61.) You can plant it, get it established, and then ignore it for a while. It's one of my favorite full-sun to light shade ground covers of all time.

Thyme has small leaves. Even the upright forms create a mounding mat on the ground. On the short side, it is just a few inches; on the tall side, it reaches about 12 inches. All thyme is highly fragrant and has masses of late spring flowers, usually pink or white. Some are more citrus in scent, while others are more medicinal.

Thyme prefers light soil that drains well, making it a perfect choice for containers and raised beds. It is drought tolerant once established. You can start thyme from seed, but I tend to pick up already-started plants that catch my eye at garden centers and nurseries. I have also been successful taking cuttings from the plants of friends and rooting them in post indoors.

After a couple years, thyme may become woody or begin dying out in the center. If that occurs, dig the whole plant up, cut apart the root ball, and replant two or three of the green, live sections. Just discard the woody center and you'll have newly revived plants. Thyme is really the perfect landscape plant—attractive foliage, pleasing fragrance, beautiful flowers, and useful in the kitchen.

POTENTIAL PESTS AND DISEASES

None; overwatering can create root rot.

HOW TO USE

If you're planning to dry thyme for using year-round or in recipes, harvest sprigs prior to blooming for the best flavor. Otherwise, I use it fresh whenever I want some—and I use it often. Fresh thyme is great sprinkled in salads, chopped in dressings, sauces, and so on. I also use it in tea or medicinally as well. Traditionally, thyme has been used for its disinfectant properties and to fight infections.

RECOMMENDATIONS

There are several colors, flavors, and fragrances available for thyme, so you should definitely plant more than one. Argentus has pretty silver-edged foliage that will catch the eye. Lemon thyme has purple flowers and variegated silver or

This Archer's Gold thyme is a brightly colored cultivar that can light up a mixed bed or border. Photo courtesy of Baker Creek Seeds.

gold leaves. Doone Valley has yellow spotted leaves and is diminutive at 5 inches tall. Hi-Ho has strong silvering and is compact. Oregano Thyme has a strong, medicinal herbal flavor. Caraway has a more upright and taller form, plus attractive rose flowers. Mother of Red has bright rose-red flowers on a short, matting plant. In addition to the several named cultivars, you could choose a darker green foliage like Woolly Thyme (*Thymus pseudolanuginosus*), which has lovely lavender flowers. French thyme or Greek thyme each have a unique look in the landscape.

This Fantastico tomato is an All-America Selection Winner and just one of thousands of varieties available for you to try. Photo courtesy of All-America Selections.

✿ Tomato (*Lycopersicon escullentum*)

Tomatoes are a classic warm-season addition to most vegetable plots. With their fast-growing vines and beautiful fruits, they look great in the landscape as well. In fact, before their fruit was found to be edible, they were grown for many years as a purely ornamental plant.

BOTANICAL INFORMATION: *Frost-Sensitive Perennial (Grown as an Annual)*

Tomatoes come in two types: determinate and indeterminate. Determinate are bush form and will usually set fruit sooner—they set their fruit for the year and then are done. Indeterminate are typically vining form and will continue to grow, produce flowers, and set fruit until the growing season is over. Both have uses in the edible landscape.

GROWING GUIDE

Plant seeds directly outdoors after the last-frost date because these warm-season plants are sensitive to winter temperatures. Germination will be best when you have temperatures over 50 degrees at night. I tend to put more than one seed in each hole, and space each planting about 1 foot apart. I can always thin the seedlings if all the seeds come up but I hate bare spots in the garden, especially in an edible landscape design where the garden is "on display."

Otherwise plant already started seedlings out in the garden. The worst mistake you can make is planting your tomatoes out too early. Pick up healthy, small seedlings that aren't too big or leggy.

If they are already beginning to flower, and you transplant them, they may not be healthy.

Tomatoes love good quality soil with plenty of organic matter mixed in, but if it's too rich in nitrogen you'll find lush, leafy vines with too little fruit. If you mulch, choose compost over manure top dressing so they get what they need without too much nitrogen. Bush tomatoes will usually need a support of some kind, and indeterminate tomatoes will absolutely need a trellis or support, and probably one bigger than you anticipate. I've seen vines grow well over 8 feet tall.

These cherry tomatoes are growing well as part of a window box garden. Photo courtesy of M. Williams, founder of A Moveable Garden.

I often train them twisted around a length of twine. We grew them along a fencerow and tied twine from the top of the fence, down at an angle staked into the ground. The tomato vine will have both flowering and non-flowering stalks—it's simple to pinch off the non-fruiting suckers. This will allow the tomatoes to develop better fruit and make them easier to train. They can also be trained up a trellis or fence as well.

Grow cherry tomatoes from hanging baskets as a gorgeous cascading fruit, if you're in an area where summer drought isn't an issue. Our area is so hot in the summer, tomatoes do better in the ground where I can mulch and help conserve water. But I adore the look of those sprays of cherry tomatoes draped from a hanging container.

Combine tomatoes with other herbs and even flowers in a large container. The contrast of color in flowers, fruit, and foliage is eye-catching and beautiful. In a container they can be a centerpiece. In a mixed border grow them up a trellis as a beautiful background for the rest of the plants.

POTENTIAL PESTS AND DISEASES

Cutworms and hornworms are some of the biggest pests tomatoes face. Hornworms eat huge amounts of leaves and fruit in a short amount of time, so hunt for them in the mornings and hand pick. Slugs, flea beetles, white flies, and aphids can all come by for a snack on your tomatoes from time to time also. Cutworms are particularly mean beasts that attack from the ground and kill your plants before you even see them. If you live in an area that is prone to cutworms, the best thing to do is to plant your seedlings with paper collars around them to prevent attack.

When it comes to diseases, most have to do with either poor stock or stressed plants. I recommend checking with your local county extension office to see what the diseases are in your area, and looking for tomatoes that have a natural resistance to those specific diseases.

HOW TO USE

Tomatoes are extremely versatile in the kitchen. Our favorite ways to use tomatoes are eating fresh and using them in salsa. **Note—leaves are not edible!** Tomatoes are in the nightshade family and the leaves and flowers are poisonous so this isn't a fully edible plant.

Tomatoes can be cooked green, but this isn't my favorite way to eat them. I love them perfectly ripe, fresh from the vine. Mmmmm . . . Expect around 20 pounds per plant on average.

RECOMMENDATIONS

Celebrity and Sugar Baby are great choices for containers. Silvery Fir Tree has unique, gray foliage. Siberia and Stupice are great early-maturing options for those in shorter growing seasons. Ozark Pink and Cherokee Purple are colorful heirlooms that do well in hot summer areas. Wild Bear Solar Flare is a very eye-catching cool red and orange striped tomato. Black Cherry forms beautiful sprays of burgundy tomatoes about 1 inch around. Yellow Pear is a golden heirloom that has a really great flavor. One of my new favorite heirloom varieties is the Vernissage series I found in the Baker Creek Seeds catalog. It is really beautifully striped and comes in orange, purple, yellow, and green colors. Trip-L-Crop is a great climbing tomato that can grow very long vines.

Winterberry is a lovely ground cover if your summers are mild enough for it. Photo courtesy of Liz West.

✿ Wintergreen (*Gaultheria procumbens*)

An ornamental woody ground cover that has beautiful, dark green leaves that are shiny and attractive. Red fall foliage and red fall berries.

BOTANICAL INFORMATION: *Perennial Shade Ground Cover*

Hardy in zones 4–9, wintergreen is a shade-tolerant ground cover that prefers cooler weather.

GROWING GUIDE

Wintergreen can be grown from cuttings or rooted suckers. Wintergreen has beautiful white flowers in the summer. The shiny green leaves are attractive all season long, and the fall foliage add another layer of color in autumn.

They don't do as well in the summer heat but are a pretty ground covering choice for shade garden areas. Provide plenty of mulch and water well during hot spells. It tolerates average soil just fine and doesn't need too much fertilizer. Add in compost each year to help replenish the soil in early spring to prepare for next year's growth.

POTENTIAL PESTS AND DISEASES

Nothing serious.

HOW TO USE

Wintergreen leaves and berries are used to create the wintergreen flavoring. Berries are used in tea, jam, and to flavor candy.

RECOMMENDATIONS

I haven't seen named cultivars but the official variety is beautiful.

"There is no season such delight can bring, As summer, autumn, winter and the spring."

—William Browne

6 The Top Layer of Your Designs — Trees and Shrubs

Trees and shrubs form the top later of your garden designs—they are taller, more permanent, and usually take longer to bear fruit. While spring-seeded annuals will grow, bear fruit, reseed, and die in a single growing season, some large trees can take as long as ten years to bear! Look for recommendations below for cultivars that will bear fruit sooner. Or think long-term about your home's landscape designs.

Trees and shrubs can set the tone for your home's landscape and create the foundation to build from. Photo courtesy of Liz West.

Caution: *I cannot tell you the agony and frustration of having to cut down a perfectly wonderful tree, simply because of its poor placement. Some trees sold as dwarfs will top out at 30-plus feet and shouldn't be planted right beside the house. Others, like pecans, have large taproots and wouldn't be wisely planted near or above sewer lines or septic tanks. The right tree in the right spot is a complete blessing. The wrong tree in the wrong spot is a nightmare.*

✿ Almond (*Prunis dulcis*)

Graceful trees that produce delicious nuts, almonds can be a lovely addition to an edible landscape.

BOTANICAL INFORMATION: *Fruit Tree*

Most almonds are hardy in a narrow range of zones 5–9. They are naturally rather large shrubs suitable for use as a small shade tree reaching 30 feet, but those big sizes are harder to harvest manually. Dwarf forms are available. Almond trees can even be grown in containers. They are frost sensitive; fruiting buds will die at 10 degrees.

GROWING GUIDE

Almonds are related to peaches and need full sun and well-drained soil. They will tolerate both rich and poor soil as long as it doesn't hold too much water on their roots. They will also be relatively drought tolerant once they are established, and they need little supplemental watering, making them a good fruit tree option for more arid climates.

Almonds bear on fruiting spurs for about 5–6 years so pruning 15–20 percent of the productive spurs each year will keep your tree bearing evenly year after year. Additional pruning to clean any dead wood, crossed branches, and to maintain an open shape will help prevent disease. Otherwise, a little compost top dressing each year is the bulk of the maintenance needed for almonds.

POTENTIAL PESTS AND DISEASES

Almonds face the same set of diseases and pests that plague peaches; however, they are generally more hardy and resistant than peaches are. Spider mites can be a problem. In most areas, squirrels can be the worst pests, harvesting most of the fruit before you get a chance to. Yikes!

HOW TO USE

Use almonds trees in the landscape as a small shade tree, accent planting, or even as a beautiful container on a porch or deck container garden.

RECOMMENDATIONS

If you live in an area that has late frosts after spring has begun, you'll want to choose a late-blooming variety to give it the best chance of fruiting. Mission and Livingston are two good late-bloomers that will cross-pollinate each other easily. All-in-One almond is one of the easiest for home gardeners with a 15 feet height and tolerates a hot summer with ease. Garden Prince is a genetic dwarf topping out at 12 feet tall with gorgeous pink flowers that look stunning in the spring. Hall's Hardy is a popular garden-sized that begins producing fruit in just a couple years.

✿ American Hazelnuts—*see Filberts in this chapter*

✿ Apple (*Malus* spp.)

Considered an American classic, apples have been cultivated in America since the earliest settlers arrived. They have been heavily bred for various regions and tastes since. There are literally thousands of choices available, some better suited for home growing than others. Try checking with your local county extension office to see which diseases are most prevalent in your region and what your average chilling hours are. Different apples need different amounts of chilling hours (the number of hours between 32–45 degrees) in order to produce properly.

BOTANICAL INFO: *Fruit Tree*

Apples and crabapples are hardy around zones 3–9 depending on the variety. Expect anywhere from 60–300 pounds of produce per tree depending on the size and variety planted. They are gorgeous in spring bloom and provide interest with the ripening fruit and interesting shape in winter, but there are challenges to overcome in growing apples.

This apple tree is a beautiful focal point in this fruitful backyard corner. Shade herbs and edibles like hostas and ginger grow underneath. Photo courtesy of M. Williams, founder of A Moveable Garden.

GROWING GUIDE

Most apples require other apples in the near area to cross-pollinate them. Even self-fertile varieties do better with cross-pollination; however, some varieties have sterile pollen and can't be used as a pollinator. The best pollinators have long blooming seasons.

Apples are usually limited in their size depending on the rootstock they are grafted to, though some are naturally dwarfed. Different rootstocks produce trees of various sizes and some are particularly well suited for the home garden. M-7 is the smallest at 6 feet tall. Bud 9, M-9, and Geneva rootstocks can all produce trees in the 8–10 feet range. EMLA 111 and G-9335 have trees 10–12 feet tall and EMLA-7 gets up to 15 feet tall. There are others still taller in semi-dwarf height ranges, but these listed will be better suited for home garden spaces.

All apples, including crabapples, are most gorgeous in the spring when they are in full bloom. Typically the flowers range from white to pink, but there are so many blossoms that the effect is stunning. Summer and fall fruit are attractive, although green apples do not stand out as much as the other colors. Choose varieties that thrive best in your area.

Plant apple trees in full sun areas with good draining soil. You will need to top-dress the soil each year with compost or well-rotted manure to feed the apple trees. Some will tolerate poorer soils. Crabapples are notorious for being less picky about their growing conditions. Planting disease-resistant varieties will help keep your apples healthy. Attracting beneficial insects and natural predators to the garden will help control pests without spraying.

Most of the maintenance required for keeping your apple trees bearing fruit well is in thinning the fruit and in pruning the trees. Most trees require pruning for good shape during their early growing years, and then lighter pruning to maintain good shape thereafter. It also helps to thin the fruit crop of apple trees so there is one apple every 5–8 inches apart. Otherwise, the tree will sometimes not bear fruit as well in the following year.

POTENTIAL PESTS AND DISEASES

Three main diseases will attack apple trees—powdery mildew, fire blight, and scab. The best offense for the home gardener is, in this case, a good defense by planting resistant varieties for the most common diseases in your area.

Pests include codling moth, apple maggot flies (ewwww), and woolly apple aphids. Light weight oil, insecticidal soap, and pheromone traps can sometimes be effective. Cleaning up old fruit from around the trees on a regular basis is also a must to prevent pests from being attracted to your yard and breeding in larger numbers there.

HOW TO USE

Goodness, if I have to tell you how to use apples, you haven't been living. Pies, juice, cider, eating fresh, sauced, and candied are just a few of the options available. We also like to slice thinly and dehydrate to make "apple chips" as a yummy snack for the kids.

RECOMMENDATIONS

There are so, so many apples. I highly recommend checking with your local county extension office, as I've mentioned, for varieties that do well in your region. Liberty is a beautiful apple that bears small fruit with stunning red and yellow skin. It is highly disease resistant but still sweet for eating fresh. Enterprise is only hardy zones 5–7 but has a crisp, tangy flavor.

Gorgeous apple blossoms put on a show every spring. Photo courtesy of Liz West.

and is immune to scab. Pink Pearl is a green-yellow apple that has unique pink-tinged flesh. Hudson's Golden Gem is said to be a beautiful apple that nearly glows in the sunlight. Ein Sheimer is resistant to scab and very heat tolerant (perfect for my area but no good if your summers are more mild). Spitzenburg or Esopus Spitzenburg is an heirloom variety originally grown by Thomas Jefferson at Monticello.

For crabapples, you have a couple directions to go—choose varieties that are highly ornamental or choose varieties that are also edible. Chestnut Crab is a great pollinator for other apples and has larger-than-average sized fruit for a crabapple. It's vulnerable to scab but withstands rust diseases. Dolgo is a great all-around crab with lots of fruit each year for jams and jellies. Hyslop bears fruit with higher tannin content and is often used in cider blends but must have its fruit thinned each year or it may begin bearing biennially instead of yearly.

✿ Apricot (*Prunus armeniaca* var. *Armeniaca*)

Apricot can be picky in the garden for many areas, sometimes more so than peaches or other fruit trees, and they can take 3–5 years to produce fruit. However, that fruit is so delicious, it's worth a try in the garden.

BOTANICAL INFORMATION: *Deciduous Fruit Tree*

Apricot is another Prunus tree that is hardy in zones 5–9. They typically grow between 10–25 feet and have a pretty, rounded form.

GROWING GUIDE

Apricots have been picky and disease prone in my area. They are typically easier to grow along the West coast. The flowers are white, pink, or red, and they bloom in early spring. New growth is often bronze colored and the summer foliage is beautiful lush green.

They typically grow like peaches, and suffer many of the same diseases and pests, but their earlier bloom times make them more susceptible to late frosts. They grow best in drier climates with high chill hours—usually 600 or more. If you're further south, look for low-chill varieties.

POTENTIAL PESTS AND DISEASES

Just as with peaches, fruit moths can be a problem. Control with pheromone traps and clean up dead fruit from the orchard to prevent over wintering. The best disease prevention comes from planting varieties that are resistant to the biggest issues your region will face.

HOW TO USE

Apricots are my favorite fruit to eat dehydrated, but probably the best way to eat an apricot fresh and juicy-ripe from the tree is to simply slice it in half and plop a dollop of whipped cream on top.

RECOMMENDATIONS

Gold Kist only needs 300 chill hours, which is great for warmer areas but only hardy to zones 7–9. Goldcot is hardy zones 4–7 and takes 800 chill hours. Moorpark is an English heirloom variety with early blooms and large fruit. Puget Gold is a popular variety with large, freestone fruit. Check with your county extension office for regional recommendations as well.

☆ Avocado (*Persea americana*)

For those lucky enough to live in warmer climates, the avocado is a gorgeous evergreen tree beautifully suited to edible landscaping. Large glossy leaves and delicious green pear-shaped fruit make this tree a rock star in the landscape.

BOTANICAL INFORMATION: *Evergreen Fruit Tree*

Avocado trees are frost sensitive and even the hardiest ones don't do well colder than zone 8 unless given winter protection. Avocado trees grow naturally 20–40 feet but dwarf varieties are available that grow about 12 feet tall. They take full sun. While the flowers are nothing to speak of, the fruit is lovely. The dwarf varieties make excellent container trees in large pots.

GROWING GUIDE

Provide avocado trees with plenty of sunlight and rich soil full of organic matter. Be sure they have good drainage, however, to prevent root rot. Be aware that manure-rich fertilizers can create a buildup of salts in the soil, especially when grown in containers, that avocado trees simply will not tolerate.

The best fruiting comes when trees are cross-pollinated between two different groups of trees—Group A and Group B. When purchasing your avocado trees, the nursery should tell you which group each variety belongs to. Sometimes trees are available with grafts from each group included so the tree you have will cross-pollinate itself—a boon when space is limited.

Avocados grow on lovely, broad-leafed trees. Photo courtesy of Michelle Bastian.

POTENTIAL PESTS AND DISEASES

Scale can be a problem in some areas, as can persea mites. Otherwise, the biggest pests are not insects or diseases, but rather larger animals that will try to steal your fruit. I have a friend who loses her harvest to squirrels almost every year.

HOW TO USE

Avocados have buttery, smooth flesh that is typically yellow-green. Many can be enjoyed fresh, combined in salads and salsas, used as the base of guacamole, and so on. It's a very nutritious and useful fruit.

RECOMMENDATIONS

Bacon is a group A flower hardy to 24 degrees while Don Gillogy is a dwarf (10 feet tall) making it an excellent Group A choice for containers. Hass has a long history of successful growth in containers. Murishige is a Group B with large, flavorful fruit.

☆ Blackberries *—see Brambles in this chapter*

☆ Blueberry, Highbush and Rabbiteye (*Vaccinium* spp.)

Please check the Blueberry, Lowbush entry in Chapter Five for general blueberry growing considerations. This section will focus on Highbush and Rabbitbush specific cultivar recommendations and need-to-know information.

BOTANICAL INFORMATION: *Shrubs*

- Highbush blueberries (*Vaccinium corymbosum*), hardy zones 4–7, typically needs 1000 chill hours.
- Rabbiteye blueberries (*Vaccinium asheii*), hardy zones 7–9

GROWING GUIDE

Highbush blueberries are the ones you traditionally think of as "real" blueberries, but Rabbiteye bushes extend the range a few zones further south. Rabbiteye blueberries tend to be smaller, but the fruit is delicious and nutritious.

POTENTIAL PESTS AND DISEASES

See Chapter 5

HOW TO USE

See Chapter 5

RECOMMENDATIONS

Highbush: Little Giant is a hybrid hardy to zones 5 and needs 600 chill hours. Northcountry is fabulous for edible landscaping with compact 2 feet x 4 feet bushes. Top Hat is a dwarf that is super cute and brilliant for containers. Sunshine Blue is self-fertile compact shrub with large blueberries and more tolerate of higher pH. Ivanhoe is a larger bush that is 6 feet tall and has beautifully large berries. Blueray has a spreading habit, can withstand hotter summers, and only needs 800 chill hours.

Rabbiteye: Tifblue is a late season blueberry with beautiful lush growth and heavy crops. Bluebelle produces berries over a long season for an extended crop. Woodard has a more spreading habit and is shorter with excellent fruit.

I love homegrown blueberries straight from the bush—nothing better!

✿ Brambles—Blackberries (*Rubus occidentalis*) and Raspberries (*Rubus idaeus*)

These woody rambling shrubs are related to roses. While they are often lumped in with vines, I put them in with shrubs. They have an open trailing nature, but they do not naturally climb on their own without support.

BOTANICAL INFORMATION: *Rambling Shrubs*

Trailing brambles are easy to grow and will need some form of staking or support to keep them from falling on the ground. They make excellent hedges, background for fences, or espaliers against walls. They can even grow successfully between two wires stretched the length of the row, about 3 feet apart. When I saw this system in use, any runners or canes that draped beyond the wires were pruned or trimmed, and the bushes grew easily to fill in the space.

Raspberries and blackberries are so delicious and so rarely available in stores. The soft berries do not ship well, so the best way to eat them fresh is to grow them yourself!

GROWING GUIDE

Plant your blackberries and raspberries in full sun to medium shade. Well-drained soil is best. While brambles will tolerate poor soil conditions, they will bear larger yields of larger fruit when the soil is enriched with some organic matter.

Staking isn't required but it can help keep the plants healthier and prevent fruit from rotting where it touches the ground. Canes grow rapidly each season, sometimes adding 10 feet or more in a single year. Fruit is produced on old wood, so let these canes grow and flower. We typically prune any wayward canes, and cut back about 1/3 or ¼ of the canes each year to keep the plants renewed and growing well.

Blackberries have cores in the middle, but with raspberries the cores stay on the plant leaving a hollow on the top of the berry. That's how you can tell at a glance which is which, even when you have black raspberries or colored blackberries. Harvest the berries when they are ripe and easily plucked from the canes.

POTENTIAL PESTS AND DISEASES

Blackberries and raspberries have few diseases and pests, especially when grown in a home garden with regular pruning and trimming to keep good airflow and circulation around the plants. Rust is a fungus that can sometimes affect the leaves of brambles. Pruning affected branches and leaves is the best control. Cane borers can sometimes be a problem as well, so dispose any dead canes pruned from your berry patch.

HOW TO USE

Ripe berries do not store or ship well, so harvest them ripe and eat as soon as possible. We freeze extra berries on cookie sheets and then pour into freezer bags for longer-term storage. I also can raspberry preserves. Blackberries and raspberries make excellent pies and cobblers as well. They are literally the taste of summer to me and worth finding space in your garden for.

These blackberries are showing off their gorgeous flowers. Photo courtesy of Liz West.

RECOMMENDATIONS

For a home garden space near a front entry, pathway, or children's play area, I recommend planting thornless varieties. Some of the heirloom varieties have a lot to offer, even with the thorns, and those are best grown where daily traffic won't be an issue, such as back fence line or hedge row area.

Raspberries hanging on the canes of these brambling vines are gorgeous. Photo courtesy of Michele Bastian.

Blackberries: Apache grows huge black berries in profusion and is disease resistant. Navaho is a popular thornless blackberry with canes that grow only 8 feet long. Logan is a thornless blackberry that produces red-violet berries and is drought resistant. Triple Crown has thornless canes that grow quite long for huge yields over a long harvesting period. Illini is one of the most disease-resistant blackberries available so if you're in an area where that's an issue, try this cultivar.

Raspberries: Caroline is an everbearing raspberry with large, red berries and great disease resistance. The small 3–6 feet cane length makes it popular for tight spaces. Fall Gold produces a yellow fruit that reblooms for two harvests a years. Canby is a great thornless raspberry that is resistant to mosaic disease. Brandywine has large purple fruits, like the tomato by the same name. Taylor is a raspberry that only produces one crop per year but over a long period of time, and is known to produce huge amounts of large, red berries.

✿ Camellia, Tea (*Camellia sinensis*)

This is the tea camellia that has been used for centuries for the delicious tea produced by harvesting the leaves and growing buds from the tips of the shrubs. It's also an attractive shrub that can be pruned to manageable size in the home garden. And of course, camellias have beautiful and fragrant flowers. Tea camellia blooms are usually white, although named cultivars exist with pink flowers. Unlike the more ornamental camellias, tea flowers are single or semi-double.

BOTANICAL INFORMATION: *Perennial Evergreen Shrub*

Camellia is one of my favorite shade shrubs. I've included it in my front foundation border design because of what it has to offer. It has evergreen color, fragrant flowers, and a preference for shade where other shrubs may struggle. Tea camellia is hardy from zones 7–9, but in protected areas (like near a house) you could probably extend that range. Tea camellia will naturally grow to 15 feet or higher; however, it tolerates pruning easily. Simply trim to maintain the size you want. Commercial plants are usually kept to 6 feet tall and wide for easiest harvesting.

GROWING GUIDE

Tea camellia thrives in shade in acidic coil with a pH 4–6. It does prefer good draining, but not dry soil. Mulch is a great way to help protect the roots from drying out. Tea grows slowly so if you want a nice foundation shrub, start with plants as close to your desired size as possible. You can also grow them in containers easily because of their slow growth rate. Basically if you provide the right acidity in the soil, and don't let the plant dry out completely, you will be fine with this slow-growing, easy-going evergreen.

You can begin harvesting tea from your shrubs in two to three years. Simply pluck the first two or three buds from the growing tips of the branches. Most plants will give you two harvests per year but in areas where growth is vigorous you may get three harvests.

Fertilization once or twice a year may be helpful. Gardeners should use acidic fertilizers like those used with blueberries. The pruning for size and harvests will help the bush develop a full, bushy appearance, which only increases the future productivity.

POTENTIAL PESTS AND DISEASES

Leaf spot disease is a problem in my area, and other regions may suffer from diseases like scale. Scale is often carried by mites, which can sometimes attack camellias.

HOW TO USE

The newly harvested leaves are dried and used to brew tea. Green tea is a modern favorite and is not only used as a drink, but also to flavor other dishes in the kitchen. Black tea is the most popular, however, and is made with a different curing or drying process than the green tea.

RECOMMENDATIONS

I really love the traditional tea camellia, but there are also a couple, more rare, named cultivars available as well. Rosea has pink flowers and the new growth is also red in color. Variegata has variegated leaves, which adds a splash of white to brighten shady borders.

✿ Cherry (*Prunus* spp.)

There are two main types of cherries, sweet cherry and tart cherry (or sour cherry). They have different growth habits and pruning needs, so I'll cover both here. Consider planting both if you can. Most climates are suited for one or the other type of cherry, so it may not be possible to grow both in your own garden. Spring blooms are stunning and would be worth planting for their ornamental value alone.

BOTANICAL INFORMATION: *Fruit Tree*

- Sweet Cherries (*Prunus avium*), zones 5–8
- Sour Cherries (*Prunus cerasus*), zones 4–7
- Bush Cherries (*Prunus japonica* or *Prunus tomentosa*), zones 2 with winter protection; otherwise zones 4–6 or 7 with shade in hottest summer areas

Many cherries are not self-pollinating. If your space is limited and you can't grow multiple cultivars, make sure you check for cherries that do not require cross-pollinating.

GROWING GUIDE

Cherries can be weak at the graft union. Staking may be required, especially in areas with higher wind speeds or no wind protection. Plant the cherries in full sun where the soil will not hold water. Cherry trees tend to be more shallow rooted so they are susceptible to drought and heaving

Cherry trees produce some of the most beautiful spring flowers. Photo courtesy of Missouri Botanical Garden.

(when freezing and unfreezing during winter lifts the roots out of the ground). A good layer of mulch can be really helpful in preventing this and keeping your cherry trees healthy.

Cherry trees generally don't require excessive amounts of fertilization—using a top layer of good quality mulch and composting once a year can be sufficient. Cherries bear fruit on fruiting spurs, so the timing for pruning can be important. Every ninja knows that the best attacks are strategically planned, after all. In humid or cool summer areas, bacterial infections can be a problem for recently pruned cherries. In those areas, postpone pruning until after fruiting in the summer when cuts will dry up and heal faster.

Bush cherries generally need less pruning because they are shrubby plants that constantly create new base shoots each year. When they get crowded in the center, cut 1/4 of the oldest shoots off right at the base to open up the center. Sweet cherries are grown best when trained to a modified central leader, to encourage height and good fruit production. Sour cherries, however, are typically pruned to an open center. In addition to pruning away dead or crossed branches, trim tall growing branches to keep the trees to a manageable, easy-to-harvest height.

POTENTIAL PESTS AND DISEASES

Birds are one of the biggest pests when it comes to cherries. We aren't the only ones who think those cherries are completely delicious! If your cherries are small enough, you can cover the trees with netting or use scary-eye balloons to dissuade the predators.

Diseases that may attack your cherry trees include fruit fly maggots, tent caterpillars, and aphids. Cherry fruit fly maggots overwinter in the ground. Lay tarps down to gather dropped fruit or rake the dropped fruit as soon as it falls from the tree to help break the life cycle and protect next year's harvest.

HOW TO USE

Cherries are flexible landscape trees. Use larger cherries to shade a patio or sitting area. Bush cherries can take the place of other large spring blooming shrubs like hydrangea, lilacs, or forsythia. Tart cherries are typically smaller trees that are great in mixed borders or containers.

RECOMMENDATIONS

Tart Cherries: Meteor is a naturally dwarfed heirloom cultivar. North Star is also a dwarf and very disease resistant, making it a good choice for wetter climates. English Morella has delicious red flesh and low-chill hour requirements. Sweet Cherry Pie™ is hardy to zone 3, self-pollinating, and reaches a compact 15 feet. It is a great option for a single tree planting.

Sweet Cherries: White Gold has a beautiful yellow fruit and is a late-blooming cherry, making it less of a target for late frosts. Black Tartarian has large burgundy fruit that is very delicious. Craig's Crimson is a mid-season cherry that is self-fruitful and is genetically semi-dwarf, making it a nice stand-alone accent tree for zones 5–10.

✿ Chestnut (*Castanea* spp.)

Large, beautiful upright tree grows about 40–60 feet tall and wide, and it bears nuts within five years. Use this in place of nonedible shade trees in your landscape.

BOTANICAL INFORMATION:
Deciduous Nut Tree

- American Chestnut (*Castanea dentata*)
- Chinese Chestnut (*Castanea mollissima*)
- Chinquapin (*Castanea pumila*)

Chestnut trees are hardy in zones 5–9 and produce pounds of nuts when the trees are mature. They require cross-pollination to bear well.

GROWING GUIDE

American chestnuts were native across much of North America until a blight spread and killed many of the wild chestnut trees. Today blight resistant varieties are making a comeback, and I hope we will see more chestnut forests in America again. The flowers are fragrant white catkins that become prickly husks later in the year. Break open the husks to reveal the nut inside, and enjoy the delicious, nutritious nuts produced.

Chestnut trees are beautiful shade trees for a landscape if you have enough time. Photo courtesy of Wendy Cutler.

Chestnuts grow with large taproots so transplant saplings with great care. The hole must be dug deep enough that the taproot is straight and free of obstructions. Do not prune the roots of chestnuts like you may with other bare-root trees. However, you can prune the leaves and branches of the tree to encourage strong root production the first year.

Eastern chinquapins, also called Alleghany chinquapins or American chinquapins, are shrubbier relations to the American chestnuts, and they grow wild throughout much of the United States. These grow only 12–15 feet tall on average and produce chestnuts similar in appearance but smaller in size.

Part of their winter hardiness is their later bloom season. White flower catkins appear in the summer, well after the danger of late frosts. Hot humid climates are less suitable, and heavy, clay soils will create rot. Otherwise, give full sun and slightly acidic or neutral soil, and your chestnuts should thrive.

Maintenance is relatively minor and consists of late summer pruning for shape and yearly applications of mulch or compost.

POTENTIAL PESTS AND DISEASES

Blight, or *Endothia parasitica* fungus, is a serious threat to nonresistant trees, which most of the native American chestnuts are. Great strides have been made in recent years to breed and hybridize resistant strains in an effort to reintroduce American chestnuts to the United States; however, trees struck with blight will not grow as tall or produce nuts. Trees planted in areas where blight has been will likely contract the disease unless you grow resistant trees. I can't stress the importance of this enough, because I don't want you to waste a decade of your life on a tree that gets killed and does you no good.

HOW TO USE

Chestnuts are one of the sweetest, most delicious nuts. Roast them, cream them, use them as butter, mix with salads or meat dishes, or just eat them fresh baked in the oven. Delicious!

RECOMMENDATIONS

All the chestnuts mentioned here have been selected and bred for blight resistance. Dunstan chestnuts are chestnut hybrids that were bred from parent American chestnut trees found thriving in the midst of a dead cluster of stricken chestnuts. The natural immunity of these parent trees has been carefully enhanced through generations of breeding to develop a tree that resists blight even when inoculated with the fungus. Larger-than-average trees, be prepared for these shade trees to reach 60 feet. Eaton is a hybrid bred for the sweet American chestnut taste and has the open growth habit of Chinese chestnuts. Auburn Homestead is a Chinese chestnut that produces 30 pounds of nuts used for baking and roasting.

✿ Citrus (*Citrus* spp.)

This orange tree serves as a beautiful backdrop for the contrasting foliage in the foreground. Photo courtesy of Liz West.

Trees in the citrus family are probably one of my biggest sources of jealousy for the limitations of my growing zone. The gorgeous landscaping trees have evergreen foliage, produce fragrant flowers, bear delicious fruit, and bring year-round beauty.

BOTANICAL INFORMATION:
Evergreen Fruit Tree

Citrus plants are generally hardy to zone 9 with a few more-hardy exceptions. Beyond that, they must be grown in containers to allow the gardener to bring them indoors during the winter. Most bear well without cross-pollination so they will fruit as single, container specimens.

GROWING GUIDE

Citrus trees prefer full sun but will often tolerate light shade. They need loam-rich soil that is well drained. Mulching yearly will keep the tree growing well and support the production of the glossy, evergreen leaves.

While many trees and shrubs are best planted in the fall, citrus trees should be planted in the spring where winters are cooler, to allow the tree a chance to establish itself before winter's dormant season. Supplement with compost or rotted manure to provide the nitrogen needed for the lush foliage. If allowed to dry out, or subjected to drought, the tree will drop the fruit to preserve the tree. Keep the tree well watered if your area doesn't get good rainfall.

In a container, more fertilization will be needed. I recommend slow-release, organic fertilizers to provide a gentle, constant source of food for the tree. Watering is important! Water as much as needed to prevent drying out.

POTENTIAL PESTS AND DISEASES

Fungal infections are more common in areas with humid summers, while pest spread bacteria infections. Citrus trees can host several pests including aphids, mites, and mealybugs. In containers, it is important to make sure you don't overwinter pests on your citrus plants and give them a foothold to infest the rest of your garden in the spring!

HOW TO USE

Citrus is known for it's delicious and refreshing juice, whether it's a glass of orange juice in the morning or lemonade in the summer. Many citrus adds flavoring and enhances dishes, casseroles, and drinks in the kitchen. I also love to use it as a light marinade over meat dishes as well. With most citrus trees, the fruits are the edible parts. However, Kaffir lime also has edible leaves, sometimes used as seasoning in Asian dishes.

RECOMMENDATIONS

Meyer lemons and Kaffir limes are two of the most commonly grown container citrus trees. Both are hardier than traditional citruses. Kumquats and mandarin oranges are also hardier and can tolerate a small amount of frost without dying. Variegated Pink Eureka is an unusual lemon; it has striped yellow and white fruit and delicious pink colored flesh. Bearss is a thorny lime that might be useful to discourage unwanted traffic through a specific area of the garden, but it's more frost-sensitive so provide protection during cold snaps. Owari mandarin is a pretty, seedless orange that has an open, spreading growth habit.

The beautiful fruits from citrus trees are ornamental as well as highly useful. Photo courtesy of Liz West.

☆ Cornelian Cherry (*Cornus mas*)

Cornelian cherry or dogwood cherry are sometimes called cornels. This is a type of dogwood that produces edible, cherrylike fruits in large amounts. Grow it as a large shrub or small tree, depending on your pruning preference and space requirements.

BOTANICAL INFORMATION: *Deciduous Shrubby Tree*

These multi-stemmed trees are hardy in zones 4–8. Use it as an accent tree, as I did in the Foundation Part Shade Design in Chapter 4, or as an informal hedge or privacy screen. They are partly self-fruitful. Those planted in hedges with other Cornelian cherries will bear more fruit per tree because of the cross-pollination factor.

GROWING GUIDE

While this tree can supposedly grow up to 20 feet tall, it is slow growing and easily pruned to a smaller size. The naturally growing trees I've seen top out closer to 12 feet. Climate differences surely plays a role in this, as well as the amount and severity of the pruning you choose to do.

The early spring flowers are bright yellow and, like witch hazel and forsythia, bloom on bare branches before the leaves appear. Replace forsythia in the landscape with these fruit-bearing trees for a simple edible landscaping swap. Its tolerance for part shade bears witness to its relation to other dogwoods, which are traditionally understory shrubs or growing on the edges of forested areas.

Once the plant is well established, it needs very little maintenance. Mulch or use a shade-loving ground cover to prevent competition from weeds. Prevent drought, especially during the first couple years, to help establish a solid root system.

POTENTIAL PESTS AND DISEASES

There are no serious pests or diseases, which makes it an excellent, low-maintenance plant selection.

HOW TO USE

I had a delicious, not-too-sweet sauce made from this fruit at a friend's house as a topping on pancakes and have wanted to plant one ever since. The fruit are very cherrylike and fall somewhere between sweet cherries and sour cherries in sweetness. They can be eaten fresh, pickled, or made into liqueur. It is traditionally used as a flavoring for sherbert desserts. Preserves, smoothies, jams, and syrups are also viable options for these usually red fruits.

RECOMMENDATIONS

There are a few named cultivars available but even wild natives are gorgeous. Nana is a naturally dwarf option that is great for smaller spaces. Flava has yellow fruit instead of the typical cherry-red, while Black Plum has dark-red fruit said to taste similar to plums. Macrocarpa and Pioneer both have larger-than-average fruit, but Pioneer has a more oblong, pear-shape.

✿ Crabapple (*see Apple*)

✿ Elderberry (*Sambucus* spp.)

Elderberry is native through much of North America and hardy in zones 3–9 depending on the variety selected. It usually has a loose, casual growth habit that lends itself beautifully to a cottage garden appearance.

BOTANICAL INFORMATION: *Woody Shrub*

Elderberries can grow from 6–30 feet tall but easily tolerate pruning, even severe pruning.

- American Elderberry (*Sambucus canadensis*)—Zones 3–8, cross-pollinate for best fruit, best berry flavor.
- Blue Elderberry (*Sambucus cerulea* or *Sambucus mexicana*)—Zones 5–9, spreading habit best for screening hedges as it will overgrow landscaped areas.
- European Elderberry (*Sambucus nigra*)—Zones 5–7, self-fertile but typically less flavorful berries.

Elderberry shrubs have an upright, loose growth habit and large, flower clusters.

GROWING GUIDE

Full sun produces the best fruit but in areas with blistering hot summers, part shade is a welcome relief. They prefer fertile soil that is kept evenly moist, but they will tolerate some drought in my experience. Prune the bushes to the size you need them to be or plant naturally dwarfed plants.

Newly developed strains of elderberries have created beautifully laced-leafed and unique color options like this Black Beauty Elderberry by Proven Winners. Photo courtesy of Proven Winners.

POTENTIAL PESTS AND DISEASES

Birds are the biggest predators of the ripe or near-ripe fruit. If you begin to lose berry clusters, you may need to put a net over the bush.

HOW TO USE

Elderberry has delicious edible flower clusters, which can be breaded and fried like squash blossoms, or used to flavor water or spirits in the spring. The berries must be allowed to fully ripen in late summer. Then they can be made into syrups, jams, jellies, or added to mixed-berry pies. They can't be eaten raw; however, I often use elderberry to make a homemade cough syrup, which keeps my family healthy during flu season.

RECOMMENDATIONS

There are a few lovely named cultivars but be aware that not all named elderberries are edible. When in doubt, check with the plant developer first to make sure it's an edible variety. York has some of the largest berries of any elderberry; the clusters will droop over on the branches they are so heavy. Nova is self-fruitful and bears heavy crops of berries. Sutherland Gold has unique, lacy foliage that begins burgundy and transforms to a bright yellow by summer. Thundercloud has dark red foliage throughout the growing season. Black Lace is another unusual cultivar that has dark purple fine-cut foliage and beautiful pink flower clusters.

✿ Fig (*Ficus carica*)

Fig trees can be grown as anything from dwarf container trees to large shade trees in the yard. Don't be fooled by their classification as a shrub—they can grow to 30 feet tall if they aren't pruned and trimmed.

BOTANICAL INFORMATION:
Large Deciduous Shrub

Fig trees are hardy in zones 8–11, but their ability to recover from winter die back encourages gardeners to stretch their boundaries a couple zones further north. Trained as a single-stem tree, they look very beautiful shading a patio chair or sitting area.

GROWING GUIDE

Fig trees need well-draining soil that isn't too rich, making them a good choice where the soil is average at best. They are also sun-lovers and need lots of sun in order for the fruit to become sweet when they ripen. Also figs must ripen on the tree because they will not ripen after harvesting.

Fig trees have lovely foliage structure, and the fruit is absolutely delicious. Photo courtesy of Wendy Cutler.

How you train your fig may depend on the climate in your area. If you are in zones 9–11 where winters are mild, a single stem, tree-like fig is fabulous. Where we stretch fig production into zones 8 or 7, we are better off growing them as multi-stem shrubs or espaliers so that if one stem dies because of winter frost, we have other stems to keep the plant growing.

Figs provide year-round interest in the landscape. Interesting bark, lush leaves, and of course that fruit. They are self-fruitful. Even if you can only fit one into your home's landscape, you should try it. Remember, they will tolerate container planting. If you get enough sun in summer to ripen the fruits, don't miss out on these treats.

POTENTIAL PESTS AND DISEASES

Depending on your climate, your challenges will be unique. Humid areas may deal with rust, while other regions have specific pests to battle. Squirrels and birds are a threat to your harvest. Netting will help foil these predators from eating your figs before you have a chance to do so.

HOW TO USE

Figs are very nutritious and sweet, but many of us have only ever eaten dehydrated figs. (Fig Newtons, anyone?) Fresh figs are amazing to eat fresh from the tree or lightly grilled with sharp cheese for an amazing contrast of flavors.

RECOMMENDATIONS

Improved Celeste is a cold-hardy fig that might be a good choice for those who will be planting in less-than-ideal climates or who will be potting them in containers. Alma and Marseilles are green-fruiting figs that may help fool birds since they don't turn brown when ripe. Black Jack has a dark fruit that ripens earlier in the summer and is naturally small for a good container plant. On the other hand, Conadria is a larger, tree-sized fig for warmer climates who want an accent plant.

✿ Filbert (*Corylus spp.*)

These large shrubs are some of the easiest nuts to grow in the home garden and worth adding to your landscape as an edible hedge or screen. If you don't have room for any other nut trees, you'll have room for these easy shrubs.

BOTANICAL INFORMATION: *Large Multi-Stemmed Shrub*

- American Hazelnut (*Corylus americana*)—zones 4–9; to 10 feet tall
- European Hazelnut (*Corylus avellana*)—zones 5–9; 15–20 feet tall

GROWING GUIDE

Both American and European hazelnuts, also called filberts, prefer fullsun to part shade and are natively found in the edges of open fields transitioning between full forests and meadows. In Europe, they were often seen as planted hedge rows dividing fields, and they still make lovely, informal hedges today. They aren't picky about their soil preferences but will not tolerate standing water or poor drainage.

Hazelnuts are attractive landscape shrubs perfect for tall hedges or privacy rows. Photo courtesy of Dave Lage.

American and European filberts benefit from cross-pollination. I recommend using more than one plant in your landscape for the best nut production. Hazelnuts naturally develop into dense thickets, so pruning for shape is some of the only maintenance that will be required. Filberts will naturally tend to bear biennially, although some crosses are less prone to this. You'll have heavier productions over 20 pounds one year, and a scant harvest the next. This, plus the better yields with cross-pollination, are good reasons to plant more than one!

POTENTIAL PESTS AND DISEASES

European filberts are more susceptible to blight, but have larger, tastier nuts. American filberts are more compact bushes and resistant to blight, but have smaller, less flavorful nuts compared to European filberts. As a result, some breeders have developed hybrids in an attempt to capture the best of both worlds. Other than the possibility of blight, the biggest contender for your nut production will be the local squirrel population.

HOW TO USE

Filberts are used internationally and have a delicious taste that complements many types of food. Common as gelato flavoring in Italy, they are also commonly combined with chocolate in dessert dishes. They are excellent combined with meats and salads as well.

RECOMMENDATIONS

Some filberts are sold purely as ornamental shrubs. Check the variety you want to make sure it will produce edible nuts. The following will all produce nuts. Barecelona is the popular commercial variety and has large nuts. Epsilon has much smaller nuts, but blooms over a long period, making it an excellent pollinator. It is also blight resistant. Santiam is semi-dwarf and has great blight resistance as well. Arbor Day is cold hardy, surviving well through zone 3. Theta is a newer blight-resistant option that has a later blooming period, extending the pollination in other varieties. Red Dragon is a unique blight-resistant variety that has contorted branches and red foliage, but unlike other ornamental filberts, it still produces a large enough crop to be considered for edible landscapes.

✿ Goji Berry (*Lycium barbarum*)

Goji berries have been used for centuries for nutritive benefits. They are also easy-to-grow as part of a lovely edible garden design.

BOTANICAL INFORMATION: *Shrub*

Growing in hardy zones 3–10, the goji berry is very adaptable. It is a sprawling, multi-stem shrub without pruning. They are self-pollinating so you can grow them in a container as single accent plants if space doesn't allow you to plant more.

GROWING GUIDE

Goji berries are usually available as bare-root and potted plants, but I've heard of people getting divisions from friends with good success. These plants are undemanding and don't typically need anything special. However, Goji berries are sensitive to acidic soil and prefer alkaline soil.

Beyond that, gojis are tolerant of average to poor soil and infrequent watering. In fact, I've included these in the Small Space Side Yard Design (pp. 62–65) where watering will be less frequent and more sporadic.

I've seen people trim and carefully prune their goji berry shrubs to create a single-stemmed tree, which is great for a single accent planting. When using it as a hedge or screen, you might prefer a multi-stemmed shrub to allow it to fill in. It just depends on what level of maintenance you want and what your goal is for the look in the landscape. To harvest your berries, tie the stems together or to a trellis to help them stay more upright.

POTENTIAL PESTS AND DISEASES

There are few pests and diseases to contend with. Birds may be a problem in beating you to the harvest, however, so be prepared to net your berries.

HOW TO USE

Goji berries can be eaten fresh, brewed in tea, or used as a replacement for raisins in baked dishes. They can be easily dehydrated for use in granola and salads during the winter months when their burst of summer flavor would be a welcome treat.

RECOMMENDATIONS

Lifeberry is a more dwarf form of the goji berry and will tolerate light shade. Sweet Selections has a grayish foliage but is larger than Lifeberry. Big Lifeberry is Proven Winners' other release that easily reaches 10 feet tall and has larger berries than Lifeberry.

Goji berries are bright red and known for their health benefits. Photo courtesy of Proven Winners.

☆ Hickory—*see Pecan in this chapter*

☆ Lemon—*see Citrus in this chapter*

☆ Lime—*see Citrus in this chapter*

☆ Maple, Sugar Maple (*Acer saccharum*)

Gorgeous shade trees with stunning fall color, these trees are tapped for the sugary sap that creates the delicious and well-known maple syrup.

BOTANICAL INFORMATION: *Deciduous Tree*

Sugar maples are hardy in zones 4–8 and are popular as landscape specimen trees. They easily grow 50–75 feet tall so plan to give them plenty of space.

GROWING GUIDE

Maple trees will tolerate a variety of soil conditions as long as they don't sit in standing water. They also tend to be more sensitive to pollution from cities and traffic. Maples won't grow as healthy in over-crowded conditions because they prefer plenty of sunshine.

The useful part of the sugar maple is the sap of the tree. The sap runs best when there is a true, cold winter with warming spring days. In moderate climates the sap won't run as easily and harvests will be poor.

Harvesting sap and cooking it down into syrup can be a time-consuming process. Taps are hammered into the tree in February or March, and the sap is collected into buckets. This sap must be cleaned and processed into order to create the syrup we are accustomed to getting from the grocery stores.

Sugar maples become gorgeous, beautiful shade trees. Photo courtesy of Liz West.

POTENTIAL PESTS AND DISEASES

While there are some pests that might attack sugar maples, they are generally hardy trees. Since we aren't harvesting fruits or nuts, it doesn't usually impact the tree too much.

HOW TO USE

Use maple syrup on breakfast dishes or desserts. Delicious and flexible, it's the most popular syrup for a reason!

RECOMMENDATIONS

Bonfire is more tolerant of city conditions and only grows to 50 feet. Apollo is a columnar tree that grows only 25 feet tall and 10 feet wide, making it one of the smallest maples to use as an accent in a small space. Fall Fiesta is a large maple that puts on a stunning fall show with multiple colors. Green Mountain also reaches 75 feet and is more drought tolerant than other maples.

☆ Medlar (*Mesipilus germanica*)

These soft fruits are almost impossible to find in grocery stores because they do not tolerate shipping; however, they are delicious and make lovely landscape specimens.

BOTANICAL INFORMATION: *Deciduous Fruit Tree*

In hardy zones 5–8, the medlar grows to about 10–20 feet tall and has year-round interest to offer.

GROWING GUIDE

Unlike most fruit trees, the season of least interest is the spring. Large, white, roselike flowers appear only after the magnolia-shaped leaves have opened. The foliage has an interesting texture, and broad tropical appearance all summer. Fall coloring is lovely, and the fruit hangs on the tree a long time, sometimes even after the leaves fall. It creates interest in early winter, although the fruit are not as attractive as other.

Plant medlar in full sun and well-draining soil and it is easy to maintain. Prune lightly when needed for cleaning dead limbs to open up the center to allow more light. Otherwise, it's an easy keeper that provides delicious fruit not otherwise available.

POTENTIAL PESTS AND DISEASES

No major diseases or pests like some of the other fruit trees.

HOW TO USE

Medlars should be harvested after the first frost and then given time to ripen. The skins will darken and wrinkle when the fruits are ripe. Just open the skin and scoop out the flesh, like a pomegranate. The pulp adds a nice flavor to sauces and creams, or you can just eat the fruit fresh.

RECOMMENDATIONS

Macrocarpa is a nice variety for home gardens because the fruits are larger-than-average. Dutch or Giant is an antique heirloom variety that has a spreading, nearly weeping habit. Stoneless keeps well and is seedless, making it easier to prepare; however, the flavor is lacking in my opinion.

✿ Mulberry (*Morus nigra*)

Mulberries are fruitful, low-maintenance trees that, while not necessarily stunning in the landscape like apples in full bloom, are easy keepers. Their biggest downside is that the fruit is messy and falls easily from the tree when it is ripe. If you plant it over a driveway or area where you park your car, you'll regret it. But if you have space in a corner of the backyard, if can be a delicious addition to the landscape.

This medlar tree is a great example of the pleasing look of the tree in the landscape. The fruit (right) isn't as attractive as the tree. Photos courtesy of Wendy Cutler.

BOTANICAL INFORMATION: *Fruit Tree*

Mature mulberries can reach well over 30 feet tall and are hardy to zones 4–8, with select varieties to zone 10. There are also multi-stemmed shrubby forms that remain small trees with little pruning needed. All mulberries are self-fertile. It may be a good choice if your landscape space is very limited.

GROWING GUIDE

Mulberries are highly adaptable trees and will tolerate a wide variety of soil conditions, competition from other trees, and part shade. I have often seen them growing wild between large oak trees as a secondary, fruiting layer in the forest. Named cultivars are often improved in form or fruit size and might be better choices for the home landscape. The fruits do not ship well. Unless you have a tree, or a neighbor with a tree, you may never experience this sweet summer berry.

Harvestable berries will be produced on this fast-growing plant within just a year or two of planting. Branches are typically slender and won't often support the weight of a ladder, so we use the lazy "shake the tree" method to harvest berries. Spread a tarp or sheet you don't mind getting stained, shake the tree, and collect the berries that fall onto the tarp. Repeat the process every three or four days throughout the season to maximize your harvest.

Can, freeze, or process your berries as soon as possible because they will not store well at all. Oh, those fleeting fruits of summer!

POTENTIAL PESTS AND DISEASES

With very few pests and diseases to worry about, mulberries are a delightfully low-maintenance fruit tree. The biggest problem will be the birds that flock to your tree to enjoy their own summer harvest. If you can call that a problem—there's usually enough to share.

TREES AND SHRUBS—THE TOP LAYER OF YOUR DESIGNS | 125

HOW TO USE

Mulberry fruit makes an excellent wine, sauce, and syrup. I also like it as an alternative to blackberries in a cobbler. I also freeze the berries and use them in breakfast smoothies during the winter when fresh fruit is harder to come by.

RECOMMENDATIONS

Black Beauty has darker reddish-purple fruits and a slight weeping habit that can be pretty. Wellington has large, delicious berries and is said to be the best for fresh eating. Sweet Lavender is hardy to zone 10b and has more firm fruit that is less likely to stain. Weeping Mulberry requires staking until the desired height is achieved and then it will cascade back to the ground.

Mulberry trees produce gorgeous, raspberry-like fruits that are born in abundance. Photo courtesy of Sprittibee Photography.

☆ Nectarine (*Prunus persica*)—see Peach in this chapter

Olive trees have attractive foliage and look beautiful in the landscape. Photo courtesy of Wendy Cutler.

☆ Olive (*Olea europaea*)

These attractive, large trees with silvery-gray leaves are a natural for a sleek modern, mission style, or Mediterranean landscape design.

BOTANICAL INFORMATION: *Evergreen Fruit Tree*

Hardy in zones 9–11, this is one of those trees I'm envious over. The only reason I don't try to grow them in containers is because of how time consuming it is to harvest and process fresh olives. They certainly aren't pick-them-in-the-morning-and-eat-them-for-lunch kind of plants. They are, however, gorgeous trees for the landscape.

GROWING GUIDE

Olive trees need full sun and will grow to a medium-large tree about 30 feet tall and wide. You can train them to a single stem with heavier pruning, or train five smaller stems to create a spreading, multi-stemmed tree. They need mild winters, low humidity, and a long time to ripen, which limits their natural range. They tolerate a variety of soil conditions as long as the soils are well draining.

Olives are extremely drought tolerant but will benefit from long, soaking waterings a couple times a year when lack of water would inhibit olive production. When the fragrant, drab flowers appear in the spring, that's a good time to water the tree. And then water again in the fall when the fruit has had a long summer to grow and is ready to fully ripen. Because they ripen over a long period of time and bear fruit on last year's growth, it's not uncommon for olives to bear heavier every other year. They grow longer branches on less-fruitful years since less energy goes into the fruit and that gives them more space to fruit the following year.

Most olives are self-fruitful; however, having a pollinator variety can be helpful, especially if you're in a less-than-ideal climate. For example, in more humid climates the trees do not pollinate themselves as well, so planting two olive trees can help boost production. The hardest thing is that olives require some chilly weather to ripen, temperatures under about 45 degrees. However, the tree is damaged with temperatures below 15 degrees.

If you plan to process your own olive oil, you could harvest the olives green or black depending on the flavor you want. You won't have to handpick them for oil production—just knock them into a tarp with a harvesting basket. If you want to eat them at the table, handpick to avoid bruising. Regardless of how you harvest, processing your olives as soon as possible will yield the best flavor.

POTENTIAL PESTS AND DISEASES

Verticillium wilt is a problem for some olive trees and usually enters through poor pruning wounds. There's also an olive fruit fly's larvae that destroys the fruit. Traps and organic sprays can help, as well as good hygiene in the orchard by cleaning up older and fallen fruit. Olive trees have shallower roots. While trees are becoming established, do not underplant around the trees.

HOW TO USE

Olives make an excellent oil that is high in all the goods kinds of fat. They are also lovely to eat as table olives, once they've been processed. Olives naturally have a bitter flavor, so pickling or brining is required to make them palatable.

RECOMMENDATIONS

Arbequina is a hardier tree that is said to tolerate winters from zones 7b–9. It also has a slight weeping growth habit. Mission is an excellent dual-purpose olive tree and is one of the original types grown in North America. It spreads to 30 feet tall and wide and is hardy to zones 8b–10. Barouni is a popular, full-sized cultivar for home-grown table olives but they have low oil content. Frantoio is a lovely oil-producing tree that reaches 20–25 feet tall and does well in zones 8–9. Lucca is a newer olive tree that is bred for high productivity. Planted in the ground, it can grow in zones 8–10, or it can do well in a container.

✿ Orange—see Citrus in this chapter

Pawpaw flowers have an unusual shape and color. Photo by Lisa Francis courtesy of Missouri Botanical Garden.

✿ Pawpaw (*Asimina triloba*)

The pawpaw tree is cold-hardy and looks like a tropical plant. The broad leaves, delicious fruit, and golden fall foliage have a lot to offer.

BOTANICAL INFORMATION: *Fruit Tree*

Pawpaws are hardy in zones 4–8 and need cross-pollination. It has a soft pyramidal shape about 15 feet tall and 8 feet wide.

GROWING GUIDE

While you can start pawpaw from seeds, they will grow better and produce faster on grafted named cultivars. Plant your pawpaws from potted, not bare-root plants, because they do not transplant well. Put them in full sunlight and well-drained soil. If they handle the transplanting, you'll be good to go after that.

Once established, they easily tolerate cool winters and hot summers. With two planted, they bear well and may require support if the fruit is too heavy. Other than pruning for size and shape, there is little maintenance required for these easy-going trees.

Pawpaws are not drought resistant. Even once they are established, they may need watering if you're in a drier climate. Be sure to protect young seedlings especially, perhaps even giving them shade during their first hot summer after transplanting.

POTENTIAL PESTS AND DISEASES

Swallowtail caterpillars prefer the leaves as food, but they rarely are present in large enough numbers to do serious damage to the trees or fruit.

HOW TO USE

Eat the pulp of the fruit fresh, or freeze it in chunks to use later. When you heat it (for canning or in pies), it will change flavor. It's best for fresh or cool dishes. Seeds and skin are discarded, but the flesh is used for many things like iced desserts, flavored liquors, and so on.

RECOMMENDATIONS

NC-1 is a cross that bears large fruit with fewer seeds. Overleese is a late-ripening variety with delicious flavor. Sunflower is reliable and forms a large tree. Shenandoah is said to be a delicious variety as well.

✿ Peach (*Prunus persica*)

Peaches and nectarines are the same species botanically. The primary difference is peaches have a gene that makes the skin of the fruit fuzzy, while nectarines have a gene that makes the skin smooth. They can be fussy and particular in the landscape, but when the stars align and you get to enjoy a fresh harvest, it's amazing.

BOTANICAL INFORMATION: *Deciduous Fruit Tree*

Peaches and nectarines are hardy in zones 5–9 as a whole, although specific cultivars vary. Peaches are typically smaller trees, reaching not more than 15 feet tall.

GROWING GUIDE

Give peaches plenty of sunlight in well-draining, neutral soil to keep them happy. They typically need a good amount of pruning to allow enough light to reach the inner branches for good fruit production. They will take

These golden summer fruits are gorgeous. Photo courtesy of Jeannie Sanders.

to being trained along a wall as an espalier very easily. Prune in early spring when the branches are putting on flowers for the quickest healing time of the pruning cuts. You can then bring the twigs indoors for early spring arrangements.

At the southern edges of the hardiness zones, look for low-chill cultivars. At the northern edges, look for cultivars that are later-blooming to avoid the spring frosts.

POTENTIAL PESTS AND DISEASES

Peaches have many diseases that can hurt them but some are easier to maintain than others. Brown rot, for example, is usually spread from old fruit left on the ground to rot. If you live in an area where leaf spot diseases are common, plant resistant varieties.

HOW TO USE

The best way to eat peaches is fresh off the tree. Mmmm… But if you find yourself with a plentiful harvest, peaches will slice and can easily. They can also be dehydrated for fruit leather, made into syrup or brandy, and frozen for desserts during winter.

RECOMMENDATIONS

Peaches: Contender is a great cultivar for late-season blooms and cold-hardiness. Harbelle is a smaller tree and is highly resistant to lead spot. Rio Grande is a low-chill cultivar with highly ornamental flowers and delicious yellow fruit. Frost also has very showy blooms and moderate chill requirements.

Nectarines: Panamint is red-skinned with low-chill hours and intense flavor. Honey Kist has high chill requirements and sweet, yellow flesh. Red Chief is highly resistant to brown rot and also has showy spring flowers.

✿ Pear (*Pyrus* spp.)

A traditional fall or holiday dessert fruit, pears are easier to grow in most home gardens than some of the other fruit trees, like apples and peaches. There are thousands of varieties to choose from so I recommend being picky with those trees you choose for your area.

BOTANICAL INFORMATION: FRUIT TREE

- Hardy in zones 4–9; some varieties are hardy to zone 3.
- European pear (*Pyrus communis*)
- Asian pear (*Pyrus x bretchneideri*)

Standard pears will typically grow 30–40 feet tall and wide, but most varieties are available on dwarf rootstock as well. Container planting or heavier pruning can keep the tree under 10 feet. Almost all pears need other varieties for cross-pollination.

GROWING GUIDE

Pear trees will tolerate having their feet wet a little longer than many of the other fruit trees I've mentioned in this chapter. Fertile soil in full sun and good drainage is the preference but they are more tolerant of variable soil than they are of variable climates. Different pears are bred and selected for different summer and winter varieties, so choose carefully the right pear for the right place.

Pears only need moderate amounts of water. If you haven't had any rain in a couple weeks, give it some water. Mulch to help preserve soil moisture and feed the pear gradually over time. Your tree will begin producing fruit after about five years. They produce on old wood fruiting spurs.

European pears ripen after they are harvested. They need to be picked when they are just starting to turn. They can keep for several weeks, even months, in cold storage. Ripen a few at a time at room temperature as desired.

Asian pears, on the other hand, do not ripen once they are off the tree. Harvest Asian pears (sometimes called apple pears) when they are fully ripe. Do not expect them to store as well as winter pears.

POTENTIAL PESTS AND DISEASES

Pears have some of the same pests as apples: coddling moths, scab, and especially fire blight. In my area fire blight is quite brutal, so the best defense is to plant resistant varieties.

HOW TO USE

Pears with good texture are perfect for eating fresh. Bake them to enhance their sweetness and combine in any manner of delicious fall or winter salads. Pears also can very well. I've found that varieties with a grittier texture are actually better once they are canned.

RECOMMENDATIONS

European Pears: Bartlett is an antique pear and, while susceptible to fire blight, is delicious. It is considered one of the best-flavored pears by many. It also serves as a pollinator for many other varieties. Seckel is a disease-resistant, naturally small heirloom tree, with easy-to-harvest fruit. Orient is a low-chill pear that is good fresh or canned. Pineapple is self-fertile and blight resistant—great for a smaller garden spot.

Asian Pears: Chojuro has gorgeous fall color in addition to spring blooms and yummy fruit. Kosui is well suited for northern zones compared to other Asian pears. Ya Li has pretty, red fall foliage and large fruits.

✿ Pecan and Hickory (*Carya* spp.)

Both pecans and hickories form large, stately shade trees easily 60 feet or taller. Sometimes they have attractive fall coloring as well!

BOTANICAL INFORMATION: *Deciduous Nut Tree*

- Hickory (*Carya lacinosa*)
- Pecan (*Carya illinoinensis*)
- Hican (*C. lacinosa x illinoinensis*)

Hicans are a cross between hickories and pecans. The goal was a more cold-tolerant pecan-like nut. They are reported to be large and tasty. They are typically fairly self-fertile, but as is often the case, will fruit better with more than one variety. With pecans, you will often see them divided into Type 1 and Type 2 groups. Planting one of each will give you the most benefit.

Hickory trees are stately and have beautiful fall foliage. Photo courtesy of Liz West.

GROWING GUIDE

Hickory and pecan both establish huge root systems, so they can be slow in bearing nuts. Even once the tree begins to bear, it will bear more as it matures. Plant them as soon as you get them. Pecans and hickories have long tap roots. Before you plant, be sure the hole is deep enough and that there are no obstructions at the bottom.

Pecans are rather drought tolerant once they are established; however, in the first few years they will need plenty of watering. The first few years, the trees are growing enormous root systems that will help it survive periods of drought later. Help trees develop a strong central trunk. Prune branches that have too narrow an angle or they may break later on. I've seen pecans lose entire limbs because the weight of the nuts pulled the branches toward the ground.

POTENTIAL PESTS AND DISEASES

Pecan scab is a disease that hinders nut production on mature trees. In commercial operations, they spray the trees to combat scab. For home gardeners, the best thing is to plant a resistant variety that will be less likely to become infected in the first place. Squirrels are often big pests as well. They are far to eager to help themselves to your harvest.

HOW TO USE

Harvest hickories and pecans as soon as the nuts begin to drop. Nuts on the ground turn rancid quickly. Hickories and pecans are both delicious nuts, but pecans tend to be easier to crack. Hickory nuts almost always require a nutcracker of some kind. Both can be used in many of the same ways—in baked goods, in pies, roasted, and so on.

RECOMMENDATIONS

Hickory: Keystone is an easy-to-crack hickory that bears well on a consistent basis. Weschke is an early-bearing tree, and Wurth has great scab resistance. Lindauer cracks into full halves, which looks attractive in baked goods.

Pecan: *Type 1*—Pawnee is naturally smaller, growing only 30 feet tall, and is an excellent pollinator. Cape Fear is a good disease-resistant variety to scab and leaf diseases. *Type 2*—Elliot is highly disease resistant and has a low-chilling requirement. Mahan bears at a younger age than many other pecans while Candy is a productive, sweet variety with excellent all-around use.

Hican: Pecans and hickory will naturally cross, and many are sterile or bear poorly. However, some of the stunning crosses are available as named cultivars. Burlington is productive and self-pollinating. Henke has smaller but full nuts and bears at a young age.

✿ Persimmon (*Diospyros* spp.)

Persimmons are an underutilized tree in an ornamental landscape. Since their fruit is the main attraction, their season of brilliance isn't spring but rather fall. The most they contribute in the spring is the fresh, yellow-green color of the new foliage. They have beautiful summer foliage, colorful autumn fruit, and interesting winter bark and form though so they have a lot to add to a landscape. And persimmons are delicious. I've included them in the Three-Season Island Design on pages 72–83 because of their value.

BOTANICAL INFORMATION: FRUIT TREE

- Oriental persimmon (*D. kai*)—hardy zones 7–10.
- American persimmon (*D. virginiana*)—hardy zones 4–10.

These trees will grow anywhere from 10–60 feet or more depending on type and rootstock.

GROWING GUIDE

Persimmons are notorious for not transplanting well. Do not disturb the roots of the tree when replanting. Place persimmons in full sun in well-draining soil and keep well watered the first year. Mulch will help as well.

Trees that bear fruit in an overabundance during their first couple years may actually stunt their root system development. Consider pruning in the spring for the first few years to keep growth to a moderate amount. You can train them to a single leader to create a stronger tree form.

Some persimmons will naturally create lots of sucker sprouts or multi-stems. Persimmons often have too-long growth that is weaker or more brittle. It will need to be shortened up to prevent breakage later.

Persimmon trees produce gorgeous, orange fruit, which will hang on the tree well after leaf drop. Photo courtesy of Steve Edholm.

POTENTIAL PESTS AND DISEASES

Where summers are dry, there are few diseases to contend with but occasionally you may have trouble with fungus. Cleaning up the old fruit will help.

HOW TO USE

Persimmons are amazingly delicious but only once they are fully ripe. They ripen on the tree after the first frost. If squirrels are a problem in your area, you can harvest them a little unripened and let them finish indoors. In a pinch, you can pop an unripened persimmon in the freezer overnight and thaw it to eat the next day, though that's not my favorite way to eat them.

Once you have ripe persimmons, you can enjoy them in so many ways. Of course you can eat them raw for sweet, smooth flavor. Use the soft fruit for a dessert pudding, bake them into cookies and bread, or mix them in with cereals and granolas. There are myriad ways to add sweet flavor to many dishes. The leaves are also used in Asia for tea.

RECOMMENDATIONS

Early Golden is an American variety that is self-fertile and has great flavor. Yates ripens earlier so it's a good choice for northern climates. Mohler has medium-sized fruit that often falls from the tree when it ripens. Asian varieties to consider in the landscape includes Hachiya, a disease resistant, commercial variety, because of its excellent flavor. Jiro has larger fruit and can be eaten when still firm.

☆ Pineapple Guava (*Acca sellowiana*)

A great evergreen shrub that bears tropical tasting fruit.

BOTANICAL INFORMATION: *Evergreen Shrubs*

These shrubs are hardy in zones 8–11 and can be grown in containers further north. Standard trees can grow 10–20 feet but can be pruned and maintained at a smaller size in a large container.

GROWING GUIDE

Plant pineapple guava in full sun to part shade in the warmest areas. It does not need rich soil to grow well; it will tolerate even poor soil. They are drought tolerant, but if things get too dry while the fruit is ripening they won't be as sweet.

Most varieties do require cross-pollination, but these plants are so fabulous in the landscape it won't be hard to find room for an extra. There aren't many named varieties and cultivars available. I especially love the attractive gray-green foliage year round.

POTENTIAL PESTS AND DISEASES

Very few diseases are a problem for this shrub. It's also less likely to be targeted by the squirrels than some of the other trees—especially your nut-producing trees—in an edible landscape.

HOW TO USE

Pineapple guava, or feijoa, is a green fruit that is sweet and tart at the same time. People compare it to pineapple with strawberry. The jelly it makes is gorgeous, but it really is amazing simply eaten fresh. The flowers are also edible and can be added to fruit salads, used to top desserts, or sprinkled over ice cream.

RECOMMENDATIONS

Nikita is a beautiful dwarf option that is self-pollinating if you're limited on space. Pineapple gem is self-fertile also but grows much larger.

Plums bear an abundant amount of fruit and are one of my personal favorites.

☆ Plum (*Prunus* spp.)

Plums are one of my favorite little fruit trees. They aren't typically long-lived, but so many forms and colors are available that you can add them to almost any landscape area.

BOTANICAL INFORMATION: *Fruit Tree*

- European plums (*Prunus domestica*)—hardy zones 4–9
- Japanese plums (or Oriental plums) (*Prunus salicina*)—hardy zones 6–10
- American plums (*Prunus americana*) and hybrids—hardy in variable zones

These deciduous fruit trees grow anywhere from 6 feet multi-stem shrubs to 20 feet tall trees.

GROWING GUIDE

Plums need full sun but will tolerate part shade. All the books say plums need good quality soil, but I've seen shrubby, stunted plums growing in sandy dried creek beds and on clay hillsides here in Oklahoma. Even with stunted, twisted growth, they produce year after year in little thickets, both totally wild and on their own. So imagine how awesome they can be with a little bit of TLC.

European plums bloom on old wood so they don't need as vigorous pruning. The Asian plums fruit on year-old wood, so prune more heavily each year to encourage growth for fruit. American plums from nurseries are usually hybridized from wild North American plums and Japanese plums.

Oriental plums tend to bloom and produce sooner, but aren't usually as flavorful. My favorite plum tree is near the ranch at my uncle's house and is an American-Japanese hybrid. The fruit isn't overly large—just bigger than a ping-pong ball—but so sweet and prolific. When the fruit is ripe, it will literally fall off the tree and into the baskets when we harvest. So delicious.

POTENTIAL PESTS AND DISEASES

Brown rot is a problem when old or fallen fruit is left to rot. Raking old plums up will help prevent the disease spread. Leaf spot is a problem in some areas as well. In general, humid conditions can make diseases worse. In those areas, you should plant resistant varieties.

HOW TO USE

Plums are hands down my favorite summer fruit to can as a sweet sauce. It's so versatile and I can do a variety of flavors with it—vanilla cinnamon spice, mint and rosemary, or orange and cloves. We use plum sauce all winter long to top ice cream, oatmeal, pancakes, and anything where I might otherwise use maple syrup for a less sugary option. Eating plums fresh from the tree is a must for summer of course, but we always harvest more than we can eat in only a week, so preserving them while we can is just smart.

RECOMMENDATIONS

Where do I start!? There are so many plums to choose from, so I highly recommend checking with a local extension office about which plums do best in your area. Keep your climate and humidity levels in mind.

European: Shropshire is a late blooming heirloom variety that begins bearing at a young age. Yellow Egg is naturally dwarfed and has large, yellow fleshed plums that are so pretty hanging on the tree. Mount Royal has dark blue fruits on a hardy tree.

Oriental: Santa Rosa is popular in the Southwest. This dark-red plum is black-knot resistant and begins setting fruit at an early age. Elephant Heart has large, heart-shaped fruit that ripens over a long season. AU-Roadside is resistant to many diseases and has excellent flavor.

Hybrid plums: Superior is a vigorous tree that may need thinning and pruning; the plums are succulent and so sweet.

These plums are ripe and ready to be harvested.

✿ Pomegranate (*Punica granatum*)

Pomegranates are beautiful shrubby trees that enjoy the heat of a long summer to bear fruit ready for harvest in the fall.

BOTANICAL INFORMATION: *Large Shrub/Small Tree*

These trees are hardy in zones 7–10. These deciduous trees have pretty fall color and highly attractive fruit.

GROWING GUIDE

Pomegranates need full sun and will not tolerate much shade at all. This is one of the reasons why it's helpful to prune it lightly to keep it opened up, allowing the light to reach the lower branches. Pomegranates also require well-draining soil. Loamy soil is best but they will tolerate less-than-ideal conditions, if necessary.

Pomegranates will split their fruits if a deluge of water is received after the fruits have already begun to ripen. Watering evenly and moderately throughout the growing season will help avoid this problem. They are quite drought tolerate once they have set their roots. They are self-fertile, so no cross-pollination is required for good fruit production.

POTENTIAL PESTS AND DISEASES

Pomegranates aren't typically disease prone. In humid climates, watch out for rot. Mites can also sometimes cause problems.

HOW TO USE

Pomegranate juice can be extracted from the seeds and used in salads, as marinade for meat, or turned into jelly and syrup. Of course there's always the classic method: break it open and eat it raw. I have fond memories of sucking the seeds right out of a pomegranate my neighbor friend and I filched from his father's tree. Our parents pretended they didn't know, but I'm sure our stained fingers gave us away.

RECOMMENDATIONS

Note: Some trees available for purchase are strictly ornamental and will not bear fruit, or will not bear well. What a waste—as wasteful as ornamental pears. Be sure you are planting a variety that provides you with delicious and useable fruit as well as the lovely small tree for your landscape. Utah Sweet has unusual pink-colored fruits. Nana is a natural dwarf form that only grows 4 feet tall. Eversweet is a cooler climate variety that doesn't have hard seeds.

Pomegranates are handsome trees with highly attractive fruit. Photo courtesy of Missouri Botanical Garden.

☆ Quince

Flowering quince (*Chaenomeles*) and European quince (*Cydonia* spp.) both bring unique offerings to the edible landscape. Quince can be a little tangy but becomes sweeter after fully ripening and processing.

BOTANICAL INFORMATION: FRUIT TREE

- Common quince (European quince) (*Cydonia oblonga*)—hardy zones 3-10a
- Flowering quince (Ornamental quince) (*Chaenomeles* spp.)— hardy zones 5–9

Both are deciduous shrubs, but European quince can be pruned and grown into a small tree around 15 feet in height.

Quince is a highly ornamental fruit tree with early blooms. Photo courtesy of M. Williams, founder of A Moveable Garden.

GROWING GUIDE

Quince requires full sun but will tolerate soil that isn't as well draining, making it useful in off areas of the landscape. It's adaptable to many types of soil and tolerates part shade easily enough. However in areas with humid summers, fire blight can be a problem. Resistant strains should be planted.

Common quince can be easily pruned to a single leader by cutting away suckers and lower branches. The growth is rather twisted and interesting, creating unique landscape appeal and winter interest. You can also train quince easily as an espalier. It needs little pruning otherwise. Indeed, too much pruning can stimulate a rush of new growth, which is more susceptible to fire blight than mature wood. Prune for shape and size and interest.

Flowering quince, on the other hand, takes more pruning after harvest and before the onset of the new year's flowers. Flowering quince is usually considered an ornamental. It has beautiful early flowers on graceful sprays that look fabulous in early spring arrangements and landscapes. The fruit is edible and suitable for jelly and jams, but isn't considered good for eating fresh.

POTENTIAL PESTS AND DISEASES

Fire blight is a real concern for common quince. Pruning away affected branches well below the dying line can help prevent the spread of disease. Coddling moth can also be a problem.

HOW TO USE

Quince harvests late in the season. In fact, some northern climates will find that while trees survive, there isn't enough sun hours to fully ripen the fruit. Harvest in the fall, sometimes after the first frost or so, when the fruit turns colored and you can smell its aroma. They should easily come loose from the tree. The fruit is usually hard like a pear or apple, but the skin can bruise easily if you aren't careful in handling. I'm sure this is one of the reasons it's not often available in the grocery store even though it's a delicious fruit. Quince will store in the fridge or root cellar up to two months. Because of the high pectin content it's perfect for creating jams and jellies. In fact, you can mix it in with lower-pectin fruits and berries to help them gel better.

Flowering quince is another matter. It is usually too astringent to ever eat fresh, even when ripe.

RECOMMENDATIONS

European: Champion is only mildly tart and bears large fruits in abundance. Pineapple is named for its fruitful taste, which lasts even after processing in pies or jellies. Kaunching is a grape-fruit size, sweet quince originally bred in Russia.

Flowering: Victory has carmine flowers and larger-than-average fruits. Super Fusion is only 4 feet tall but produces prolific yellow fruits. Cameo has pink double flowers instead of the typical bright-red single flowers. It also has prolific fruit for jelly making.

✿ Raspberry—*see Brambles in this chapter*

✿ Rose (*Rosa* spp.)

A classic cottage garden shrub, roses have been grown and bred for thousands of years. The flowers and hips are edible and high in vitamin C. But the ornamental value of roses in the landscape cannot be underestimated.

BOTANICAL INFORMATION: WOODY SHRUB

Generally the older heirloom roses produce the best hips.

- Dog rose (*R. canina*)—hardy zones 3–10
- Rugosa rose (*R. rugosa*)—hardy zones 3–10
- Apple rose (*R. villosa*)—hardy zones 5–10
- Prickly rose (*R. acicularis*)—hardy zones 2–9
- Gallica rose (*R. gallica*)—hardy zones 3–9
- Damask rose (*R. damascena*)—hardy zones 3–9

Roses are self-fruitful and have beautiful summer flowers. Most roses traditionally bloom in one flush, but hybrids can bloom for longer periods or in multiple flushes of blossoms. Many modern varieties bred only for blooms, however, do not produce rose hips. As ninja gardeners, we want to find those roses that will give us the best of both worlds—rose hips *and* gorgeous blooms.

Here, Harlow Carr, a David Austin rose, blends beautifully with lavender in the landscape. Photo courtesy of David Austin Roses.

Roses are so versatile in the landscape. Rootstock and different growth habits give us the ability to have everything from tiny shrubs a couple feet high to huge climbing roses 20 feet high or more. Most fall in between as medium-large shrubs or moderate climbers.

I also want to mention a group of roses that I really enjoy—English roses. Davis Austin roses have bred hybrids between tea and bedding roses and the old-fashioned roses to create amazing varieties. The goal is to keep the large bloom, delicate charm, and heavy fragrance of old-fashioned roses that also has the repeat blooming and color variations of the tea and hybrid roses. Some English roses also have excellent flavor and produce great rose hips as well.

GROWING GUIDE

Roses typically prefer full sun, although they sometimes prefer to keep their feet in the shade. Roses in the Alba and floribunda hybrids tolerate more shade. Individual cultivars may also prove to do well in part shade conditions. I love to stretch the possibilities in the edible landscape whenever I can.

The following highlighted shrub roses are much lower in maintenance than the horror stories of tea roses you've heard about. We aren't growing show roses—we are growing amazing landscape roses that produce beautiful flowers, and more important, stunning rose hips. Pruning will happen in the earliest spring before the leafy growth begins. In these cases, you'll prune away dead or diseased wood and canes that cross each other as needed for shaping.

Fourth of July is my climbing rose, which produces one large and several small flushes of flowers, as well as small rose hips.

I have a large climbing rose. Now that it has established for five or six years, I periodically trim back one or two of the oldest canes to ground level so there's plenty of growth lower down. With shrub roses you really don't have to prune every year—easy, easy maintenance. Once your shrub roses are established, they are fairly drought tolerant as well.

Do not deadhead your roses in edible landscaping. Remember—we want the rose hips to develop. With reblooming shrub roses, we won't need to deadhead for them to rebloom. Roses combine well with so many other plants and herbs they easily mix into the edible landscape no matter what your style and aesthetic.

Another consideration is the amount of thorns and where you place the roses. Our climbing rose has huge thorns and serves as a home for birds to build their nests. It's fine for growing over an arbor by the side gate because we kept it pruned out of the pathway. However, near a sitting area or garden bench or kids' play area, I might go for a rose that doesn't have such prickly thorns. There are a few "thornless" varieties worth considering for these situations.

POTENTIAL PESTS AND DISEASES

Many of the diseases that plague other roses aren't as prevalent with the hardier roses I'm focusing on here. Japanese beetles can still be pests because they will eat buds before they open. Aphids in warm climates are always a possibility as well as some leaf diseases like black spot. Cleaning up debris and planting resistant varieties is a great defense.

HOW TO USE

Roses can be used in many places in the landscape. Tree roses are grafted at the top of long steam and so bloom in a poof at the top. They make amazing vertical accents in a garden island bed. Shrub roses are the most common and make excellent hedges, like what I used in the fruit and herb corner. A single rose will be an excellent accent, and a climbing rose looks great on any sturdy structure. I recommend planting climbing roses on sturdier, more substantial structures so they don't visually overwhelm, or physically collapse, a smaller trellis or fence.

CAUTION: Many garden roses are treated with pesticides and chemicals you should not be ingesting. Never eat roses where you don't know the history of how they've been treated. Also note that organic rose treatments often contain sulfur, which some people react badly too—use caution in what you put on roses you plan to eat.

Rose petals are edible. The more fragrant roses seem to have the best flavor. Rose petals have been used to create jelly, flavor butter, honey, spirits, and desserts. Different roses have different flavors. The darkest red roses seem to be more bitter to me. It helps to cut out the white end of the petal because that part connects to the center and is often the most bitter. The rosey pink colors are my personal favorites. They can be dried and used in many tea blends as well. Chamomile, rose petals, and lemon balm is a great blend you can make 100 percent with edible landscaping plants.

Rose hips are really awesome in not only adding fall interest, but for their usefulness as an herb. High in antioxidants and vitamin C, rose hips are a nutritious addition to your edible landscape. The pulp from inside the rose hips can be made into a soup (strain out the seeds) or preserves. The outside of the hips can be dried for tea, or you can grind it and add as flavoring to creams and desserts. One of my favorite marmalades uses rose hips as a major ingredient. So yummy.

Rose hips can be dehydrated and enjoyed year round from a winter harvest. Photo courtesy of Alfred Diem.

RECOMMENDATIONS

Rugosa roses and the dog roses have the most flavorful rose hips. Alba is a white blooming rugosa with good-flavored petals and prolific, generously sized hips. Frau Dagmar Hartopp is a smaller rose reaching just 3 feet tall with single, pink roses. Kiese is a dog rose hybrid with really pretty red-orange hips that are a welcome spot of color in the fall.

Climbers—Fourth of July, a fun climber with large thorns, has fragrant red-and-white striped petals and profuse hips, although they are small. Kew Rambler grows best with some support and has rosy-pink blooms. Westerland is an apricot blooming climber that can be great for warm-colored gardens.

English or hybrid roses—Scepter'd Isle, a fragrant David Austin rose, has gorgeous pink flowers. I chose it for my Fruit and Herb Corner Design on pages 67–71. Scarborough Fair has pink, semi-double flowers on short, upright canes. Belle Story has pretty, cup-shaped apricot-to-light-pink blooms on 4 foot shrubs.

✿ Sweet Bay (Bay Laurel, Grecian bay, *Laurus nobilis*)

This pretty evergreen shrub grows as a small tree in certain climates and provides an easy-to-maintain culinary contribution to the edible landscape. California bay is a close relative but has been known to cause allergic reactions in some people.

BOTANICAL INFORMATION: *Evergreen tree*

Hardy in zones 8–11, sweet bay can be grown as a container plant in cooler zones and overwintered in a protected location. I show it in a container in Front Yard Foundation Design on pages 41–45.

GROWING GUIDE

True sweet bay is a Mediterranean plant that takes lots of sun and well-drained soil. They will take part shade, especially during the dry heat of summer. These multi-stemmed trees will grow to 15–40 feet naturally, but many dwarf forms are available. They also grow slowly and can be easily grown in containers. Prune them to keep their smaller stature.

Sweet bay is not a heavy feeder. With a yearly mulch application, fertilizer is rarely needed. The plant is beautifully fragrant and lends an attractive air to any garden design. The thick foliage cover makes it a good choice for a hedge if you live in an area where it grows in the ground.

Sweet Bay is perfect for containers in zones north of zone 8. Photo courtesy of Proven Winners.

POTENTIAL PESTS AND DISEASES

Few pests bother this aromatic tree, although occasionally leaf damage occurs from tiny aphid-like insects.leaf damage occurs from tiny aphid-like insects.

HOW TO USE

Bay leaves can be used fresh, but the flavor is the strongest after the leaves have been allowed to dry. Dehydrate the bay leaves out of the sunlight until they are crispy and then store them in an airtight container until you need them.

RECOMMENDATIONS

All Grecian bay trees are attractive in the landscape. There are some varieties or named cultivars worth considering though. Angustifolia has longer, more narrow leaves. Crisp a has undulated, crinkly leaves, and Aurea has leaves tinged in yellow. Sicilian Sunshine has gorgeous, golden foliage when it leafs out and is a pretty contrast to a typical green.

☆ **Wolfberries—*see Goji Berries in this chapter***

"We gardeners are healthy, joyous, natural creatures. We are practical, patient, optimistic. We declare our optimism every year, every season, with every act of planting." —Carol Deppe

7 Edibly Ornamental — Perennials, Biennials, and Annuals

Ornamental edible plants make up the bulk in your landscape, and they will fill your garden with beautiful tasty goodness. Some of these plants are clearly edible (broccoli, for example), while others are complete ninja secrets (like hostas). Enjoy the exploration of possibilities as you plan your own spaces!

Cottage garden borders like these are a brilliant mix of edibles and ornamentals. And some plants are surprisingly both! Photo courtesy of Wendy Cutler.

☆ Amaranth (*Amaranthus* spp.)

Amaranth is a delightful plant for the edible landscape. It's colorful and has multiple edible parts.

BOTANICAL INFORMATION: *Warm-Season Annual*

Amaranth forms the bright red background of this sensory garden space. Fennel's fine cut foliage and curly leaf kale are in the mid-ground, and nasturtiums are just visible in the foreground. Photo courtesy of M. Williams, founder of A Moveable Garden.

GROWING GUIDE

Amaranth is a leafy green that has gorgeous seed tassles as well. Love-Lies-Bleeding has been planted for years purely as an ornamental plant, a hold-over from its inclusion in cottage kitchen gardens. The colorful greens are quite edible, especially if you harvest the tenderest leaves. The seeds that are produced are also edible and very high in protein.

Plant seeds a couple weeks after the last front and keep them moist until they sprout (usually a little over a week). Thin them to a foot apart. Once it's established, it is one of the most drought tolerant greens.

Amaranth grows anywhere from 18 feet tall to 5 feet tall depending on the variety. It can look more informal when allowed to go to seed, but the foliage is as brightly colored as coleus. Best of all, it's a green that will tolerate the summer heat much better than most lettuce and cabbage. This is closer to malabar spinach in heat tolerance but much more colorful.

POTENTIAL PESTS AND DISEASES

Cucumber beetles are one of the only pests that bother amaranth, and usually only when the plants are young. You can cover them with netting until they are past the seedling stage to protect them.

HOW TO USE

The leafy greens are simply harvested and enjoyed as desired. They make great additions to salad and to stir-fry dishes. You can sauté them like spinach with minced garlic and sea salt.

The seeds that develop on the colorful tassels are high in protein—a really great quality protein high in amino acids. Use it like oatmeal-style porridge or roast it. What you don't harvest, the birds will.

RECOMMENDATIONS

Joseph's Coat is a gorgeous tri-colored heirloom grown in Monticello's gardens. The plant has yellow, red, and bright green foliage and will grow to 4 feet tall. Dreadlocks is a pretty 3–4 feet selection with bright fuchsia flower sprays that have an unusual weeping habit. Green Thumb is a dwarf form with bright green foliage and flower spikes that stays under 18 feet tall. Aurora Yellow have dark green, light green, and bright yellow foliage that stands out in the garden.

✿ Asparagus (*Asparagus officinalis*)

Asparagus is a lovely perennial vegetable that is far too often overlooked for its amazing landscaping potential. The ferny fronds are gorgeous, but will die back during the winter. I used these in the Three-Season Island Design on pages 73–83.

BOTANICAL INFORMATION: *Perennial Vegetable*

Asparagus is hardy in zones 2–9.

GROWING GUIDE

Asparagus, a perennial plant, will bear for over a decade. Even though you can find it in the grocery store (at an expensive cost), it's so much better tasting when it is harvested fresh from the garden. Asparagus is usually planted as established roots and they are often very long. While we make sure the asparagus bed is full of great, friable soil with plenty of organic matter, we always make sure the holes for planting are deep enough to hold the soil well.

Asparagus ferns are highly attractive, lacy fronds. Photo courtesy of Anne Heideman.

Asparagus is a heavy feeder. We mulch the patch well with compost and well-rotted manure. We also keep a thick layer of mulch over the entire patch to smother out any weeds that would steal nutrients from the asparagus plants. You may tend to neglect asparagus once you've harvested it in early spring, but if you baby the fronds just a little bit, you'll have bigger harvests in the future.

The spears appear straight out of the ground in early spring. See page 142 for details about harvesting your asparagus. You may not be able to harvest any the first year—that is normal.

During the summer and fall, enjoy the gorgeous ferny fronds. They are so beautiful, if a touch leggy. In my Three-Season Island Design on pages 72–83, I make sure there are herbs and edging plants in front of the asparagus to help hide the leggy bottom portion. Asparagus will appreciate a light fertilizer like seaweed or fish emulsion during the summer growing season. In the fall, after the fronds die down completely, cut them at ground level and place them on the compost bin.

POTENTIAL PESTS AND DISEASES

Asparagus beetles are a pest that attacks asparagus. Break the cycle of wintered eggs and larvae by cleaning up the fall fronds and not letting them sit on the ground once they die back. In humid summer areas, asparagus may not perform well.

HOW TO USE

Simple is best for fresh asparagus. We love to drizzle it with olive oil, sprinkle it with rosemary and thyme and a touch of garlic salt, and grill it. So good.

RECOMMENDATIONS

Mary Washington is a popular heirloom variety with long spears. Jersy Giant is an all male hybrid well-suited for colder climates. Purple Passion has sweeter-than-average spears that are burgundy purple in color. UC 157 is a hybrid developed in California for extra heat tolerance, so while it isn't hardy in cooler seasons, it is better for southern zones.

✿ Basil (*Ocimum basilicum*)

Basil is one of my favorite herbs. It's grown easily from seed, available in many colors and shapes, and prolific as long as the sun is shining.

BOTANICAL INFORMATION: *Annual*

GROWING GUIDE

Basil is a true sun-loving annual. It will not germinate well until the soil is warm enough, and even then its germination rate isn't fabulous. Don't be afraid to be generous the seeds. Any seedlings you thin can be tossed into a salad or sandwich, so it won't be wasted.

Basil loves the sun, but hates drought. Take care to water it more than many of the other herbs you might have in the landscape. I grow them in containers so I can water them directly. You can pinch off flower spikes to encourage bushier growth of the leafy foliage, which is the part you harvest, but I often forget or even intentionally let them flower because they look so pretty. Basil doesn't need a lot of extra fertilizing and will grow well in containers.

POTENTIAL PESTS AND DISEASES

Very few pests or diseases.

HOW TO USE

One of the most popular ways to use basil is, of course, pesto. But that's just the start when you have access to plenty of fresh basil close at hand. Basil is excellent with any tomato-based dish, in sandwiches, mixed with pasta salads, and added to regular salads for an added zing. I love basil and, when it's available in the summer, use it all the time.

RECOMMENDATIONS

Blue Spice is one of the most strongly scented basils and has attractive, deep purple foliage. Siam Queen is an All-America Selection winner with large, attractive leaves and pretty flower spikes. Holy Basil has green and purple foliage with a unique mint flavor overtone. Dwarf Greek Basil has small boxwood-like foliage and a pleasant rounded growth habit. Lime has bright-green colored foliage. Lemon is named not for its color but for the citrusy fragrance and flavor. Cinnamon has a very unusual spicy, cinnamon flavor. Nufar is a hybrid basil with enhanced disease resistance.

I love that basil comes in a beautiful variety of colors, like this rosy purple basil. Photo courtesy of Alfried Diem.

☆ Beans

Here I will discuss the unique beans not covered in Chapter 5: garbanzo beans (also called chickpeas), and fava beans or broad beans (uniquely cold-hardy).

BOTANICAL INFORMATION: *Evergreen tree*

- **Garbanzo beans** (*Cicer arietinum*)
- **Fava Bean** (*Vicia faba*)
- Beans, Pole and Bush (*Phaseolus vulgaris*)—See Chapter 5
- Scarlet Runner Beans (*Phaseolus coccineus*)—See Chapter 5
- Lima Beans (*Phaseolus lunatas*) —See Chapter 5
- Long Beans (*Vigna unquiculata var. sesquipedalis*)—See Chapter 5
- Asparagus Bean or Winged Bean (*Psophocarpus tetragonolobus*)—See Chapter 5

Note: Fava beans have been known to cause allergic reactions in some people. Use caution if you don't know whether you are allergic or not.

GROWING GUIDE

Garbanzo beans should be planted in full sun after the danger of frost has passed; however, fava beans can be planted much sooner, when you plant peas in the early spring. If you've never grown beans in the area before, inoculate with a purchased "bean inoculant" to help the roots fix nitrogen more effectively.

Fava beans have a pretty, upright growth habit that makes them useful in the mid-levels of the garden. They will grow well in the garden until the temperature reaches 75 degrees. Fava beans, like peas, will tolerate some frosty cold snaps, so it makes a good fall garden choice as well.

Garbanzo beans are bushy, short plants that reach about 18 feet tall and wide. Chickpeas have pretty shallow root systems so moderate, regular watering will be important. They are usually ready to be harvested about 100 days after planting. They are nice for filling space in a summer container that can be put away and stored during the winter. I grew them in containers on my back porch in our old home and they were lovely in spring and summer while we were outside during warm days.

POTENTIAL PESTS AND DISEASES

As with most legume family-members, blight, mosaic leaf diseases, and fungus can be a problem with beans. Do not replant beans in the same space year after year or you'll encourage the spread of disease.

HOW TO USE

The most common way to use chickpeas is to grind them into a paste as hummus. They also make an excellent addition to stews and chilies. Fava beans or broad beans can be harvested like snap beans. Let them mature further and harvest as shelled beans. They are ready for harvest about 85 days from planting and can be used fresh, canned, or in soups.

RECOMMENDATIONS

Fava: Windsor is an heirloom variety that's been around so long that people sometimes call fava beans Windsor beans. Aquadulce is a Spanish heirloom that produces large white beans. Negreta is an Italian variety with purple beans.

☆ Bee Balm (*See Monarda*)

☆ Borage (*Borago officinalis*)

These charming blue flowers are edible and bought themselves a place in my Small Space Side Yard Design on pages 62–65 because of their usefulness and beauty.

BOTANICAL INFORMATION: *Annual*

GROWING GUIDE

Borage is a flowering herb that was often seen in cottage gardens and kitchen gardens. The flowers are edible and have a cooling, cucumber taste. The large leaves are a fuzzy gray that combines nicely with other plants in the landscape. The leaves are also edible, especially when harvested young. Plants typically grow no more than 2 feet tall and wide.

Since they don't typically transplant well, start borage by seed in the spring after danger of frost. They don't require any special soil to be happy and actually tolerate quite poor soil. They grow quickly, as most annuals do, and give you blooms by the start of summer.

Borage flowers have a graceful look to their gorgeous blue flowers. Photo courtesy of M. Williams, founder of A Moveable Garden.

The flowers are blue star-shaped flowers and have a sweet, nodding charm in their clusters. Harvesting the flowers as they appear will encourage additional flowering. If you allow the flowers to set seed before the fall is over, you will find that it often self-sows in the garden and new volunteers will appear. The flowers will attract many pollinators to the garden.

POTENTIAL PESTS AND DISEASES

Very few, if any.

HOW TO USE

Borage leaves develop a fuzz on them as they mature. To use in salads and herbal teas, harvest while they are still tender and smooth. Borage flowers can be harvested any time and are used in teas, lemonades, wines, and more. Historically borage was used to bolster courage. The flowers are also known to trigger lactation in pregnant and nursing women, so should be avoided during those times.

RECOMMENDATIONS

There really aren't many named varieties of borage; however, you can sometimes find both white and pink flowers plants if you prefer those over the blue. Blue is such a unique color in the garden landscape that I used the traditional blue borage.

☆ Brassicas (*Brassica oleracea*)

Broccoli, cabbage, kale, and cauliflower are all cool-season annuals that do better in the late winter/spring gardens or planted at the end of summer for fall gardens.

Brassicas are stars of the fall landscape and provide many edibles. Photo courtesy of Liz West.

BOTANICAL INFORMATION:

- Broccoli (*Brassica oleracea var. italica*)
- Broccoli Raab (*Brassica rapa var. rapa*)
- Cabbage (*B. o. var. capitata*)
- Cauliflower (*B. o. var. botrytis*)
- Kale (*B. o. var. viridis, B. o. var. acephala*)
- Mustard (*B. juncea*)

Even though cabbage and broccoli seem like different vegetables in the kitchen, they grow in much the same way in the garden. Cabbage is especially beautiful in an edible landscape as it is available with cool crinkled leaves (called savoy) or in purples and reds. I find, however, that cabbage is less quick to bolt compared to broccoli and is easier for me with my too-fleeting springs. It does seems to attract more pests to the garden, however. Cauliflower is grown just like broccoli. Kale is the easiest keeper of the group, and will tolerate more heat than broccoli, cabbage, or cauliflower. It's also frost tolerant. Mustard can be a colorful, highly attractive addition to the fall garden and fall containers.

GROWING GUIDE

Sowing outdoors requires a longer spring period. If I plant brassicas in the spring, I start the seeds indoors. Yet I can easily start seeds outdoors in late summer for a fall garden. If your springs are milder and longer you may have no trouble. Kale and early maturing cabbages seems to do best for me in the spring while broccoli and cauliflower are much better producing in the fall. Mustard can begin to be harvested in just a few short weeks.

All brassicas are heavier feeders, so they will not object to rich compost being added to the soil where they are being planted. If you plant them in the same area more than once, you'll want to amend the soil again. When I interplant cool-season veggies with warm-season annuals (and I often do), I don't rip up the plants when they are spent. Instead, I cut off the plants at ground level and put them in the compost bin.

Provide plenty of water since shallow roots don't delve as deep for water. Mulch generously to help conserve water as well.

POTENTIAL PESTS AND DISEASES

The pests for all are much the same—numerous. Army worms, slugs, cabbage worms, and flea beetles (just to name a few) all snack on the leaves. Root fly eats the roots of the plant and kill off a plant that otherwise seemed to be doing just fine. Clubroot is a fungal root disease. Avoid this by rotating where you plant brassicas in the garden. Mustard has fewer pest problems.

HOW TO USE

Broccoli is harvested by cutting of the young flower clusters before they open to reveal the yellow blooms inside. Cauliflower is the same. Some broccoli forms a single large head but many heirloom varieties form side shoots providing multiple harvests. Broccoli raab is grown for the zesty greens and should be harvested before the flower shoots open.

Cabbage is harvested as needed, or when rounded heads have completely formed. Kale is one of the sweetest of the group and harvested fresh for salads. If you've never had homegrown kale, you don't know what you're missing.

RECOMMENDATIONS

Broccoli: Di Ciccio is an Italian variety that has lots of edible side shoots when the first bunch has been harvested. Packman matures early and is perfect if your season is shorter. Arcadia is very cold tolerant so it has time to form a large head in the fall garden. Waltham is a popular heirloom variety for good reason—lots of side shoots makes it productive for the home gardener.

Cauliflower: Fremont is a self-blanching cauliflower so you don't need to do anything fancy to make it appear white. Cheddar has a yellow-orange instead of white color. Graffiti has a true purple color, making it attractive and unusual in the garden.

Cabbage: Early varieties do best in the spring where they can quickly mature before summer's heat ends the season. Arrowhead has a small size but attractive appearance. Early Jersey Wakefield is an heirloom variety that was once grown commercially and is sweet tasting. Black Palm Tree has loose leaves in a deep, black-green. Mid-to-late varieties take a little longer and, in my area at least, do better in fall gardens. Perfection Savoy has pretty crinkly leaves on compact plants. Scanbo is disease resistant and also stores well. Savoy King is an All-America Selections winner that is reported to have very good flavor.

Kale: Toscano also known as dinosaur kale or Lacinato has oblong, savoyed leaves that are attractive in combination with other plants, and tolerates heat well. Winterbor is very cold hardy and will regrow for prolonged harvests. Redbor has gorgeous deep burgundy leaves and grows nearly 3 feet tall. Scarlet has deeply curled and savoyed leaves that are red tinged and very beautiful.

Mustard: Japanese Giant Mustard is so beautiful, large, and multicolored that it works as a stand-alone plant in a container. Southern Giant Curled has beautifully savoyed leaves and is heat tolerant. Green Wave has frilly, curled leaves that are very interesting in the landscape. It's both heat and cold tolerant.

☆ Broccoli—*see Brassicas in this chapter*

☆ Cabbage—*see Brassicas in this chapter*

☆ Calendula (*Calendula officinalis*)

These cheerful, warm-colored flowers have been part of the cottage garden for centuries because of their edible blooms, beautiful flowers, and ease of growth.

BOTANICAL INFORMATION: *Hardy Annual*

GROWING GUIDE

Calendula grows easily from seed if you direct sow around the last frost date, although you can usually find potted plants at nurseries in the spring and fall. That should tell you something about their temperature preference— cool! Once summer heats up, they are replaced by sun lovers like sunflowers or zinnias, but during the uncertain weeks of spring and fall, they are the rock stars.

Calendula prefers soil on the slightly rich side, but like many of the other pollinators we've talked about in this book, they want well-drained soil. Containers are a great

Calendula's beautiful flowers and usefulness in the kitchen have earned it a place in the cottage garden for hundreds of years. Photo courtesy of Colleen Codekas, Founder of GrowForageCookFerment.com.

place to grow them. If you do not harvest all the flowers from the plant, it is likely they will reseed themselves. The seeds will probably survive the winter and then pop up in a preferred place in the garden.

POTENTIAL PESTS AND DISEASES

Powdery mildew can be a problem, especially in the dwarf forms, if they are overcrowded. Don't be afraid to thin the seedlings as needed to give plants their space.

HOW TO USE

Calendula has many uses both for wellness and in the kitchen. The edible flowers are zesty and add flavor and color to winter soups and salads. I've also seen them mixed into omelets and fried rice dishes, or used as a substitute for the more expensive saffron.

In herbal medicine, the calendula flowers, harvested when they are sticky, are thought to have anti-inflammatory and antiseptic properties. Calendula is usually applied topically in salves, oil infusions, or even in tea skin washes.

RECOMMENDATIONS

Pacific Beauty is a single blooming form on a taller, 2–3 feet stem. Though not a true white (but as close as you can get with calendula), the tall and buttery yellow flowers of Double White Shades make good cut flowers. Orange King have huge double blossoms. Pink Surprise, apricot-pink colored, grows 18–34 inches. Bronzed Beauty is a pretty light-peach color bloom with bronze-colored back, giving the flowers a cool two-toned effect.

✿ Cauliflower—*see Brassicas in this chapter*

✿ Chamomile, Roman (*Chamaemelum nobile*)

Chamomile is a perennial herb that is an easy keeper in the garden and makes a relaxing tea.

BOTANICAL INFORMATION: *Perennial Herb*

Roman Chamomile is true chamomile and is a hardy perennial for zones 4–9. German chamomile or sweet false chamomile is *Matricaria recutita* (or sometimes *M. chamomilla*) and is a warm-season annual.

GROWING GUIDE

Chamomile can be grown from seed or from cuttings of the parent plant. It prefers well-drained soil that isn't too wet or rich. In fact, it seems to put on more blooms in poor soil than in rich soil!

Historically it's been used as a companion plant of choice for many other vegetables and herbs, so it is well suited to the blended garden situation of an edible landscape design. The plants grow only about 12 inches tall and are usually low maintenance. Harvesting flowers often will encourage new blooms and extend your harvest period.

POTENTIAL PESTS AND DISEASES

None

HOW TO USE

Chamomile is most famous for it's soothing tea; however, you can also dry the blooms to add to sachets and pillows to improve sleep. Chamomile blends as easily with other herbs in the kitchen as in the garden—add the petals to salad, tea blends, and other dishes with lemony herbs to enhance their flavors. I like to add them to a bath when my skin is irritated from heat.

Chamomile adds open growth habit and airy foliage to the garden. Photo courtesy of Alfred Diem.

Note—Chamomile is related to the ragweed. Those who have allergies to ragweed may also have allergies to chamomile.

RECOMMENDATIONS

German chamomile is said to be sweeter in flavor for use in salads and single-flower teas, but it is an annual and will need to be replanted each year.

✿ Chives (*Allium scheonoprasum*)

These members of the onion family are so beautiful in the landscape! They are one of my favorites for edging, mixed borders, or containers.

BOTANICAL INFORMATION: *Perennial*

Hardy to zone 3.

GROWING GUIDE

Chives grow easily from seed sown just a scant 1/8 inch, but they will take a year before they are big enough to be substantial in the landscape or provide plenty of harvestable greens. It's best to start from potted plants if possible, to give yourself the head start.

Chives will grow 10–12 inches and have flowering spikes around 2–3 feet tall, depending on the variety you choose. Chives will tolerate part shade, so they mix in well as an edging in the shadier parts of Transitional Space Design on pages 36–40. I love their thin, grasslike foliage and use them as I would ornamental grass in the garden design and in mixed containers.

Chives have strappy foliage that blends well with other plants in the landscape. Shown here with yarrow. Photo courtesy of M. Williams, founder of A Moveable Garden.

The greens have a mild oniony or garlic flavor. The flowers are also edible and have a stronger flavor. Sometimes they can be used as garnish only. You can cut back the entire clump if it starts to look messy in the summer and it will renew the leaves. Deadheading flowers will help encourage the production of more and prevent reseeding if you don't want them sending up volunteers.

POTENTIAL PESTS AND DISEASES

Aphids will sometimes attack the foliage, but they are relatively pest-free plants.

HOW TO USE

Both the leaves and the flowers are edible and add a mild garlic or onion flavor to a variety of dishes. Anywhere you might want to add a sweet onion taste, you can add chives or blooms: omelets, stews, baked potatoes, pizza, stir-fry, salads, sour cream, vinegar infusions, and more.

RECOMMENDATIONS

There are dark-purple, pink, and white chives available. All are pest-free and easy-to-grow.

✿ Cilantro (*Coriandrum sativum*)

Cilantro and coriander are the same plant but used in different ways. Cilantro is the zesty leaves of the plant, often used in salsas. Coriander is the dried seed of the plant and used as a spice.

BOTANICAL INFORMATION: *Cool-season Annual*

GROWING GUIDE

Because cilantro will bolt quickly once things warm up past 70 degrees, start seeds indoors well before the last frost date. Alternatively you can scatter seeds outdoors where desired in the fall. It's a definite cool-season plant and prefers mild temperatures. As summer heats up, shading helps to extend the harvest of leaves, but ultimately once the soil warms up, it will quickly produce a flowering stalk.

If you allow the flowers to grow and set seed, you can harvest the seeds as well! Once the plant grows its flower stalk, the leaves become much more bitter. Tie a paper sack around the top of the flower stalks once they begin to dry out or you will lose the seeds. But don't worry—any that fall to the ground will probably produce volunteer seedlings in the future.

POTENTIAL PESTS AND DISEASES

Very few, if any.

Cilantro's fine cut foliage here makes a nice contrast to broadleaf lettuce in the background and the growing vegetable seedlings in the mid-ground.

HOW TO USE

SALSA! Oh, sorry, did I shout? Seriously though I love salsa of all kinds and cilantro is the secret sauce for salsa magic. Use cilantro primarily as a fresh herb for uncooked dishes because cooking weakens the flavor.

Coriander is a spice that's often used to season sausage. It's also great in winter-baked bread, mixed with beans, or to season stews.

RECOMMENDATIONS

There aren't really named varieties to purchase but if you have a gardening friend who has been growing cilantro and saving the seeds themselves, you might get some from them. These regionally bred plants may be hardier to your unique growing conditions.

Comfrey's broad leaves look attractive naturalized here with lavender and other herbs. Photo courtesy of M. Williams, founder of A Moveable Garden.

✿ Comfrey (*Symphytum officinalis*)

Comfrey is a perennial herb with a robust root system that makes a great addition to a naturalized landscape, but it requires caution in allowing it to naturalize where it may not be wanted.

BOTANICAL INFORMATION: *Perennial Herb*

Hardy in zones 4–9, comfrey grows about 4 feet tall and 2 feet wide.

GROWING GUIDE

Comfrey can be grown from seeds but is most often available in starts or cuttings from other gardens. They are often used to naturalize fruit orchard areas because their large root system paves the way for shallower rooted fruit trees, drawing nutrients and moisture up to the surface. You can periodically mow them and allow the leaves to fall as a natural mulch.

Comfrey grows in full sun to part shade so it's quite adaptable. Comfrey doesn't take much water, and it's nice for low-maintenance areas. Once they are well established in an area, they can be hard to uproot so be sure you want them where you put them.

POTENTIAL PESTS AND DISEASES

Comfrey has very few pests and diseases, although snails and slugs can sometimes nibble on the leaves.

CAUTION: While comfrey was historically used as an internal herb, recent studies have shown potential liver toxicity. I'm including it in the edible landscape directory because of its usefulness and ease-of-growth in naturalized areas, but it shouldn't be consumed internally.

HOW TO USE

Comfrey is prized for its coarse leaves, which are used in external applications such as poultices for bruising, sprains, and strains. Comfrey-infused oils are used in skin creams as well.

RECOMMENDATIONS

Comfrey is in the borage family. Its flowers are often pink, blue, or white.

✿ Daylily (*Hemerocallis* spp.)

One of the most cheerful edible flowers is the daylily. I adore these flowers in the edible landscape. Literally thousands of color, shape, and size options are available to you.

BOTANICAL INFORMATION: *Hardy Perennial*

Hardy to zones 3–10.

GROWING GUIDE

Plant daylilies in the early spring or fall. You'll get more blooms with a fall planting; however, the daylily grows so robustly that you'll probably get blooms the first year. Subsequent years will have larger and larger blooms as the plant matures. Daylilies can be divided every 4–5 years to keep them growing healthy.

Daylilies grow in full to part sun. As long as they get about 5–6 hours of sunlight, they tolerate many kinds of soils and conditions. Plant on an unusable slope or in low-maintenance areas that you don't water or tend to often. Water well the first year to establish, but after that they are pretty easy keepers.

Some daylilies keep their foliage green all year round. In cold winter climates this can create a mushy, untidy mess, but in my area the winters are usually mild enough that they still look good. If you're in a very cold winter area, you may choose the deciduous daylilies so you don't have to trim back the foliage each year.

POTENTIAL PESTS AND DISEASES

Very few pests or diseases.

HOW TO USE

Daylily buds are traditionally used in stir-fry dishes and in spicy soups. They can also be baked or roasted like asparagus! Harvest daylily buds the day before they are ready to open for the best flavor.

Ruby Spider daylily is just one example of the amazing varieties that are available. Photo courtesy of Proven Winners.

Some varieties are quite sweet, while others taste like green beans. Some have a metallic, bitter aftertaste, so taste them before you decide which ones to plant.

Opened flowers can also be eaten if you remove the pistils and stamens. Stuff them like peppers or squash blossoms. Or slice them and add them to salad and soup.

RECOMMENDATIONS

Some of the heirloom varieties are so unique that they are worth preserving in the garden. Hyperion is a tall, popular, yellow heirloom—over 3 feet tall in the garden and great for the middle or back of mixed border. Ophir is another large, yellow antique daylily with deep trumpet-shaped flowers. Potentate has gorgeous raspberry-purple blooms on medium-sized plants.

Daylilies produce lots of buds that are also edible. Photo by Lisa Francis, courtesy Missouri Botanical Garden

CAUTION: Some people report allergic reactions to daylilies. As with all edibles, you should use caution whenever you try something new for the first time. Just because something is edible for most people, doesn't mean it's going to be edible for you.

Cottage pinks mix well with other plants in the landscape. Photo by Lisa Francis, courtesy of Missouri Botanical Garden.

✿ Dianthus (*Dianthus* spp.)

Dianthus or pinks also go by the name Sweet William or cottage pinks. There are lots of common names for these amazing flowers.

BOTANICAL INFORMATION:
Herbaceous Perennial

Hardy to zones 5–9

GROWING GUIDE

Pinks take average soil and full sun and need well-draining soil. They are usually available as cuttings or divisions and should be planted in spring or fall.

These perennial flowers are highly attractive in the edible garden landscape. They have gray-green foliage that blends well with a variety of plants, and the blooms are beautiful. They don't love the hottest summer days but will typically bloom both spring and fall.

POTENTIAL PESTS AND DISEASES

Very few pests and diseases

HOW TO USE

They have a clove-like fragrance and flavor, but, of course, different varieties have different flavors. Most of the petals improve their flavor if you cut away the white edge where they connect to the center of the flower. They look amazing in salads, are great additions to soup and stew, and even can be added as flavoring to spirits and jellies.

RECOMMENDATIONS

Sweet William (*D. barbatus*) has gorgeous coloring but very little fragrance. Clove pinks (also called edible carnations; *D. caryophyllus*) have a light, spicy fragrance and flavor that is surprisingly sweet. *D. plumarius* has more ornamental flowers that have sweet, nutmeg flavor.

☆ Dill (*Anethum graveolens*)

Dill's foliage is not only gorgeous but also edible and useful in the kitchen.

BOTANICAL INFORMATION: *Cool-Season Annual*

GROWING GUIDE

Plant dill in the spring or sow directly outdoors in the fall in warmer climates, like zone 7. Thin seedlings to 10–12 inches apart and provide plenty of nutrients.

Dill is a tall herb reaching 3 feet or more. The fine-cut foliage makes it a fabulous choice for use as a filler plant in the border. Trim foliage on a regular basis—not only to harvest the awesome edibles but also to encourage bushier growth.

Dill flowers are gorgeous umbels of yellow blooms. They attract many pollinators and swallowtail butterfly caterpillars. Water moderately for the best growth. Let the plant set seed at the end of the season for volunteer plants in the future. Or save some of the seeds for used as digestive aids.

POTENTIAL PESTS AND DISEASES

Dill will bolt if it gets too dry, so mulch to prevent bolting.

HOW TO USE

Dill foliage is a classic for baked potatoes, pickles, and other dishes. The seeds are great for relieving bloating and upset stomach.

RECOMMENDATIONS

Hercules has a lot of foliage and is a large plant. Fernleaf is a compact 18 inches but still has beautifully fine-cut foliage. Any dill will do amazing in the garden though.

Dill flowers are highly ornamental and also attract many pollinators to the garden. Photo by Lisa Francis courtesy of Missouri Botanical Garden.

These echinacea are growing in a beautiful city landscape display in New York. Photo courtesy of M. Williams, founder of A Moveable Garden.

✿ Echinacea (*Echinacea purpurea*)

One of my favorite low-maintenance perennials of all time, echinacea also happens to be a useful herb.

BOTANICAL INFORMATION:

There are several echinacea varieties; however, herbalists favor *E. pupurea* so that's what I'm discussing here. *E. angustifolia* is the other commonly medicinal variety. Hardy to zones 3–8.

GROWING GUIDE

Echinacea can be grown from seed if you give them a chilling period of two weeks or more. They can take a few days to show up, so keep the soil moist until the sprouts appear. Once they are established, they are highly adaptable and tolerate a wide range of soils. Anything except extremely fertile or clay-ridden soil that prevents good drainage is perfect. They thrive in poor, well-draining soil and don't need much watering once established.

Echinacea will naturalize in good climate conditions and can be divided after a few years if you aren't harvesting the roots.

Roots are used in herbal preparations. Usually when herbalists harvest the roots, they will leave smaller side roots to continue growing. This eliminates the need for traditional divisions.

Echinacea flowers resemble black-eyed Susan daisies and are commonly available in purple, mauve, pink, white, or orange. I adore these plants! They work so well in a wide variety of garden designs. I use them in the Mailbox Planter Design on pages 46–48 because of their low-maintenance easy care.

POTENTIAL PESTS AND DISEASES

Very few pests and diseases, but soggy roots may cause rotting problems.

HOW TO USE

Herbal tinctures are made from the roots of the echinacea. Echinacea is used to boost the immune system; however, resistance builds up after prolonged use. Use echinacea when you're actually sick for a few days and then stop using it for a few weeks. I would grow this plant regardless—it's one of my top flowers.

RECOMMENDATIONS

Alba is a white variety, as the name implies, and is variable in size. Bright Star has large, upright rose-purple flowers. Green Envy is highly unusual with dark green centers and two-tone petals—pink with lime green edges. Lilliput is a Terra Nova released dwarf that stays under 18 inches tall.

Echinacea blooms are large, graceful flowers for any garden landscape. Photo by Liz West.

Ruby Giant is a bright pink flower on a much taller plant with huge, 6-inch wide flowers. Vintage Wine has burgundy purple flowers and grows 2 feet tall. Sparkler is a new variety that has unusually variegated foliage—medium-green with white mottling throughout. I could go on all day. You seriously cannot go wrong with any echinacea varieties.

Fairy Tale Eggplant is a gorgeous eggplant perfect for containers. Photo courtesy of All-America Selections.

✿ Eggplant (*Solanum melongena*)

Eggplant is in the nightshade family, so only eat the fruit.

BOTANICAL INFORMATION: *Warm-Season Annual*

GROWING GUIDE

Eggplant needs a warm growing season. Start the seeds indoors 8–10 weeks before the last frost date. They transplant easily into the garden, provided they have enough moisture. Otherwise, you can start with seedlings.

Eggplants are handsome shrubs with beautiful fruit. They have a tropical look with their broad leaves and beautiful purple fruits. I love planting them in stand-alone containers or mixed containers where the fruit is more at eye level.

They require full sun for best fruit production, like tomatoes and peppers. Eggplants need a long growing season. Northern climates may not have a full 2–3 months of long growing days needed to ripen the fruit. Eggplants are heavy feeders so amend the soil well.

POTENTIAL PESTS AND DISEASES

Flea beetles, mites, aphids, and whiteflies can all be pests. Eggplants are susceptible to the same diseases tomatoes have and should not be planted with them in the garden. Growing in containers where you can change out the soil can help prevent that.

HOW TO USE

Eggplants are very versatile fruit! Many Italian dishes use eggplant in them. Grilled eggplant is stunning, and they are excellent in vegetarian lasagna and yummy cheesy baked dishes.

When it has reached its full, mature coloring, it's ready to harvest. Cut the fruit off the plant carefully so you don't disturb the other growing fruit.

RECOMMENDATIONS

Fairy Tale is a dwarf eggplant with maroon-purple and white streaked fruit. Rosa Bianca is an Italian heirloom that takes almost 80 days to mature but has large, delicious white and lavender fruit. Neon has bright magenta-purple fruit that is long and skinny. Zebra has dark-purple fruit with white streaks in it.

✿ Fennel (*Foeniculum vulare*)

Fennel has gorgeous foliage, similar to dill, and is delicious in the kitchen.

BOTANICAL INFO: *Biennial grown as annual*

GROWING GUIDE

Fennel can be started indoors 4 weeks before the last frost, and it will self-sow in future. Fennel is touchy about transplanting so I use biodegradable pots to plant them outdoors and not disturb the root system.

Fennel doesn't need a ton of mulch or fertilizing. But they need even watering so they don't bolt.

POTENTIAL PESTS AND DISEASES

The biggest pests for fennel are the caterpillars that like to munch on the leaves. One year we had several swallowtail caterpillars on one of my fennel plants. We were happy to sacrifice the one plant in exchange for being able to watch the beautiful butterflies hatch from their chrysalis later in the season.

HOW TO USE

The seeds can be used as seasoning. The foliage is used to garnish dishes and it adds a soothing, relaxing element to teas. In bulbing fennel forms, the bulbs can be harvested.

RECOMMENDATIONS

Bronze fennel has gorgeous, purple-copper foliage that reaches over 5 feet tall. Florence fennel has a thicker bulb stem and is more compact at 2 feet tall. Orion is a bulb form with large, crisp bulbs.

✿ Feverfew (*Chrysanthemum parthenium, Tanacetum parthenium*)

Cute, daisy-like flowers used historically to repel insects and in herbal medicine.

BOTANICAL INFO: *Perennial*

Hardy to zones 5–8

GROWING GUIDE

Sow feverfew seeds directly outdoors in the cool of early spring. Super simple—just sprinkle the seeds where you want them and don't bother covering them up. Sunlight is necessary. Just mist the ground lightly to keep the soil moist while the plants are sprouting and becoming established.

Feverfew can become a little leggy over time, but if you harvest and cut them back, that will help. Loam soil is best but feverfew plants are highly adaptable to a variety of situations. Their cheerful, daisy-like flowers are gorgeous.

Feverfew is a perennial. After fall frosts kill it off, just cut back the plant. It should reappear in the spring. It also may reseed itself and provide volunteer plants to share with friends. They will bloom from mid-summer until fall's frosts, providing you with tons of useful plants for the herb garden.

POTENTIAL PESTS AND DISEASES

Very few!

HOW TO USE

Feverfew helps repel insects in the garden and has traditional wellness uses also. It was used not only as a digestive aid but also to relieve migraines and headaches.

RECOMMENDATIONS

Feverfew can often be obtained from divisions or seedlings from other gardeners. Check with other herb gardeners to see what they have in their gardens and you may be able to save yourself some money!

✿ Hosta (*Hosta* spp.)

Surprisingly edible, these shade garden favorites were originally grown and bred for the tender spring shoots.

BOTANICAL INFO: *Perennial*

Hardy to zones 3–8

GROWING GUIDE

Hostas tolerate a large amount of shade and have been bred in a variety of colors, shapes, and sizes. Originally they were bred and developed for their edible shoots. They've since been hijacked as purely ornamentals by many landscapers, but they are delicious and can be a perfect perennial edible for a shady garden area. These could easily be substituted for some of the other plants in the Front Yard Foundation Design on pages 41–45.

Hostas are usually purchased as potted plants or dormant crowns with roots. Plant them quickly in fertile soil that will support the growth of the lush foliage. Hostas are often divided after 2–3 years, so you might be able to get starts from a friend!

Keep them well watered until they are established; however once they are established, they will not be particularly drought tolerant. Too much sun will burn variegated leaves or bleach the deep-blue color of some varieties.

Hostas leaf out late in the spring. I find myself always wondering if they didn't make it, and then they magically appear as shoots of leaves getting ready to unfurl. Once they leaf out they form wide, mounding clumps, which are attractive. Flowers are white or purple, tube-shaped, and born on tall flower spikes in summer. The foliage is definitely the highlight of these flowers. They look lush and amazing for months, until winter frosts kill it back.

Clip away and compost dead flower spikes and foliage during the winter to prevent pests and disease from overwintering.

POTENTIAL PESTS AND DISEASES

Slugs and snails are one of the biggest pests you'll be contending with. Bait, traps, and exclusion barriers like a ring of diatomaceous earth or wood ash sprinkled around the plant can help combat these pests.

HOW TO USE

In the landscape, hostas are brilliant for shade gardens and understory layers. In the kitchen, it's the tender, leafy shoots that you're after. Cut the leafy spears just like asparagus (to which they are related), and cook in much the same way. I had an amazing sushi roll that was wrapped around hosta spears once and it's surprisingly asparagus/cucumber like. I've also seen them baked with bacon and garlic. Once the leaves begin to unwrap, they will be tougher and increase in bitterness. Do not harvest more than 1/3 of the spears from any clump in a given year. I usually harvest the larger spears from the outside and leave the smaller inner shoots to grow.

RECOMMENDATIONS

Hostas are available in a huge variety of shapes and sizes, which enhances the contrast and beauty in the garden. Sum and Substance grows to a huge 6 feet tall and wide with deep blue-green leaves. Great Expectations is one of my favorites! It has bright yellow leaves edged in medium green and grows 2 feet tall and wide. Golden Tiara is also green and yellow but this medium-small hosta has yellow edges on green leaves. Patriot is a popular, smaller hosta with white edges on green leaves. Vanilla Cream has bright chartreuse-green leaves that have a heart-shaped appearance. Tiny Tears grows only 6 inches tall and has bright-green arrow-shaped leaves.

These shoots can be harvested like asparagus spears for tender spring edibles. Photo courtesy of Jeannie Sanders.

These Blue Cadet shoots show a much darker blue-green color and form a large, mounding clump of foliage in a shade garden. Photo courtesy of M. Williams, founder of A Moveable Garden.

✿ Kale—*see Brassicas in this chapter*

✿ Lavender (*Lavendula* spp.)

Lavender is surprisingly edible—a pleasant bonus for any plant that is so stunningly gorgeous. Lavender's purple flowers are so sweet and airy and fragrant, and the foliage is gray enough to mix well with any landscape design.

BOTANICAL INFORMATION: *Hardy Perennial/Shrub*

Hardy to zones 5–9

GROWING GUIDE

Lavender can be grown from seed but it takes awhile to reach maturity. Sow seeds in a cold frame in early spring, or outdoors in the fall in milder winter zones. You can also root cuttings of the growing tips in the summer when new growth is being quickly put on.

Once the perennial is established, it is very drought tolerant. It needs full sun to stay happy. It's perfect for a low-maintenance border or an area that won't be tended as often, like the Mailbox Planter Design on pages 46–48. Lavender grows generally around 2 feet tall but different varieties are available both taller and shorter.

POTENTIAL PESTS AND DISEASES

Very few pests or diseases. The main thing that kills a lavender plant or makes it sickly is if the soil holds too much water.

Lavender flowers are graceful and the gray foliage blends well in the landscape. Photo courtesy of Missouri Botanical Garden.

HOW TO USE

Lavender is best harvested when the flower spikes are just beginning to open, in the morning before the heat of the day exhausts the plant. Flowers can be plucked from the stems for some purposes, or sometimes the entire stem is cut. Lavender-infused oils are used in everything from soaps to cleansers to beauty preparations. The fragrance is calming and soothing and used for a variety of wellness applications. The varieties suited for culinary purposes are often added to teas and desserts and gourmet dishes.

RECOMMENDATIONS

English lavender (*L. angustifolia*) is one of the varieties most commonly prized for in medicinal purposes. It is one of the sweetest-flavored flowers for use in the kitchen as well. It's also the hardiest, tolerating as far north as zone 3 with winter protection. Hidcote has deep-purple flowers and grows 18–24 feet tall. Munstead is a classic lavender popular for good reason. It's brilliant as a border plant and prized for its long bloom time. Silver Strands has silvery gray foliage on mounded bushes 18–24 tall and wide. French lavender or lavandin (*L. intermedia*) is a sterile hybrid that is fragrant like English lavender but tolerates summer heat and humidity better. Provence is one of the most popular lavandins and is considered great for culinary use.

✿ Lemon Balm (*Melissa officinalis*)

Lemon balm is one of the most useful plants in the mint family and lends not only beauty to the landscape but also citrusy delight to the kitchen.

BOTANICAL INFO: *Herbaceous Perennial*

Hardy to zones 5–9. Can be grown as an annual north of zone 5.

GROWING GUIDE

Sow your lemon balm directly in the ground or plant transplants in the spring. Alternatively you can take divisions or plant starts in the fall. Lemon balm will easily spread and naturalize throughout.

Related to mint, lemon balm will tolerate part sun conditions, making it a nice understory herb for fruit trees or large shrubs. The plant will quickly reach 2 feet tall unless you pinch it back from time to time as you harvest leaves. The flowers are not overly showy but are highly attractive to pollinators in the garden.

POTENTIAL PESTS AND DISEASES

No real pests or diseases. It can be somewhat invasive.

HOW TO USE

The flowers are edible and can be added to lemonades, wine, or other drinks for a mild, lemony flavor. The leaves are much more concentrated with the burst of lemon flavor, however, and are more often used. For eating, they are added to fish or chicken dishes or used in stir-fry. Teas or infusions made from the leaves are thought to be uplifting and soothing.

RECOMMENDATIONS

All Gold has yellow-lime colored foliage. Aurea or Varigata is a variegated yellow-green on medium-green coloration. Compacta grows only about 6 feet tall and doesn't bear flowers.

✿ Lemongrass (*Cymbopogon citratus*)

A great substitute for ornamental grass in the landscape, lemongrass has a rich, citrus fragrance and is a common addition to teas.

BOTANICAL INFORMATION: *Herbaceous Perennial*

Hardy to zones 9–11; grown as an annual elsewhere.

GROWING GUIDE

Propagate from divisions or sow seeds after danger of frost has passed in the spring. It will not grow well in temperatures under 50 degrees, so bring it indoors to overwinter or replant in the spring, depending on your preference.

The foliage looks like long grasses but is fragrant when it's bruised or crushed. As the plant matures, it develops thicker stems at the base of the foliage. These are used in many stir-fries and dishes to add lemon zest. At a fully mature size, one lemon balm will reach 3 feet tall and wide. In my garden (zone 7), we grow it like an annual or take a division indoors to replant in the spring.

POTENTIAL PESTS AND DISEASES

No real pests or diseases. The only concern is frost.

HOW TO USE

The stalks add an amazing flavor to stir-fry, curry soups, and other exotic dishes.

Lemongrass is a lovely substitute for ornamental grasses in the landscape. Photo courtesy of Missouri Botanical Garden.

RECOMMENDATIONS

Lemongrass doesn't have named cultivars and varieties, but the main species plant is beautiful and useful in it's own right.

☆ Lettuce (*Lactuca sativa*)

Lettuce comes in so many more colors and shapes than what you see in the grocery store. If you aren't used to the beautiful reds, limes, speckled, and variegated options available, you may be surprised to see lettuce here. But ninjas know that there's usually more to a plant than meets the eye.

BOTANICAL INFORMATION: *Cool-Season Annual*

There are four primary groups of lettuce:

Crisphead lettuce—the type you see at the grocery store like Iceberg. It's the most heat tolerant so it's perfect for spring gardens.

Butterhead lettuce—Loose leaves with a semi-heart at the base helps make this lettuce more drought tolerant.

Romaine—No heart like crisphead or butterhead, but an upright, pretty form that would be more formal in a border or edging.

Loose leaf—The most variable type with bunches of floppy leaves that can be harvested individually instead of as a single group.

GROWING GUIDE

Sow lettuce seeds outdoors in the spring when temperatures reach about 40 degrees. You can start seedlings in a cold frame as well and them transplant them. In the fall, wait for temperatures to reach about 70 degrees before sowing seeds to get the best germination rates.

This cinnamon lettuce is just one example of the colorful lettuces available for edible landscaping. Photo courtesy of Baker Creek Seeds.

Lettuce is fairly easy to grow and most will grow rather quickly. Water evenly to avoid bitterness. They will appreciate a good layer of mulch to conserve moisture and smother out weeds.

They reach maturity quickly. Even those slow to bolt will come out of the garden soon enough. You can interplant them with a warm-season annual so that when lettuce is finished, something else is ready to take its place. Or you can replant new lettuce seeds every couple of weeks to make sure you fill in the gaps.

While most say lettuce needs full sun, I say afternoon shade is welcome in hot summer areas. Lettuce combines well in containers with other annuals and edible flowers.

POTENTIAL PESTS AND DISEASES

Because lettuce is grown for its broad, luscious leaves, it is no surprise that most of the pests that attack it are coming after the leaves. Aphids and slugs love to snack on your lettuce almost as much as you do.

HOW TO USE

I hardly have to tell you how to enjoy lettuce, except I will say this: if you've never grown your own salad before, you do not know what you are missing. Eating a salad won't feel like a side note to the meal. It will be the main attraction and something you look forward to. Pinky swear!

RECOMMENDATIONS

I highly recommend beginning with some old-fashioned heirloom and antique varieties. Look for unusually colorful or beautifully shaped. Flame has, as you might imagine, edges with a bright red, and the variety is growing in popularity. Rougue d'Hiver, a lovely purple-burgundy-tinted lettuce, is heat and cold tolerant. Lolla Rossa is an Italian variety with frilly red leaves that would add a unique foliage texture to the landscape. Tom Thumb is a cute dwarf lettuce that reaches only 4 inches tall and wide. Winter Marvel has a pale-green head and great cold tolerance. Flashy Butter Oak has oak-shaped leaves with a light-green background and red speckles evenly throughout the leaves. Australian Yellow has very savoyed leaves in dazzling yellow-green and is more heat tolerant. Cimmaron has oblong leaves because of its romaine type, but they are a glowing red color.

✿ Mint (*Mentha*)

Mint is one of the most recognizable fragrances and is such a useful plant in the kitchen. It's brilliant to add it to the edible landscape as well.

BOTANICAL INFORMATION: *Herbaceous Perennial*

Hardy to zones 3–10, mint grows anywhere from 6–36 inches depending on variety.

GROWING GUIDE

Mint is easily grown from cuttings and divisions. You can also grow it from seed, but once it's established it is easy to create cuttings. In fact, mint spreads quickly so many gardeners confine it in containers to prevent it from overtaking an area.

Mint can become quite leggy if allowed to grow unchecked. Trim back the growing tips of the plant when you harvest to encourage bushier growth. The flavor of the leaves will deepen when the flower spikes appear; however, I do not find it unpleasant by any means. I harvest the mint I want to store before the flower spikes appear, and then I continue to use the mint fresh for as long as possible.

POTENTIAL PESTS AND DISEASES

Whiteflies can be a problem for mint, especially in areas with bad air circulation. Leaf rust can be a problem in overcrowded or humid conditions.

In this photo, spearmint and chocolate mint make a pleasing combination.

HOW TO USE

Mint is a classic addition to many beverages and is used as a stand-alone tea or in many blends. It also makes an excellent addition to many dishes, including fresh salads, salsas, and ice cream. Mint jelly is also amazingly versatile.

RECOMMENDATIONS

Mint comes in several varieties, usually named for the flavor variations that they have. Chocolate Mint has a true chocolate overtone that I absolutely adore in ice tea. Ginger is ginger-flavored and has dark-green leaves. Curly mint has upright, curled leaves, with such a unique foliage texture for the garden. Peppermint is a classic mint and the plant that is used for the extract in candies and desserts. Variagata has white and green leaves. Apple Mint has a rich fruity flavor I really like for many dishes as well.

✿ Monarda (*Monarda didyma*)

Bee balm, Oswego tea, and Bergamot are all names that this gorgeous flowering herb has been called. It's a testament to the popularity of the plant throughout the ages.

BOTANICAL INFORMATION: *Herbaceous Perennial*

Hardy to zones 4–9.

GROWING GUIDE

Seeds can be sown in the spring. They also grow well from cuttings and divisions. Bee balm is a fast-growing plant and will reach its full height of 3 feet the first year. Plan to divide clumps when they get old after about 3 years.

Monarda grows well in full sun to part shade. The flowers have a unique starburst of tubular petals that attract bees and hummingbirds. While the traditional variety is a gorgeous red color, there are cultivars available in a wide range of colors from blush-pink to purple.

POTENTIAL PESTS AND DISEASES

Powdery mildew is a problem in nonresistant varieties.

HOW TO USE

Monarda makes an excellent tea, adding a sweet, tangy flavor to your blends. Both leaves and flowers are usable in the tea, although the flowers are more strongly flavored than the leaves. The leaves and young growing tips are edible in steamed dishes or soups.

RECOMMENDATIONS

Adam has bright red flowers and is more tolerant of dry soil conditions than other bee balm plants. Grand Mum has huge, mauve flowers that are very full. Pardon My Purple has a darker pink-purple bloom on a dwarf 12-inch tall plant. Snow White is a large bee balm that reaches 3 feet tall and produces gorgeous creamy-white flowers. Jacob Kline is a crimson red flowering bee balm that is mildew resistant and good for humid climates.

Bee balm attracts pollinators to the garden. Photo courtesy of Patrick Standish.

☆ Mustard—*see Brassicas in this chapter*

☆ Oregano and Marjoram (*Origanum* spp.)

Marjoram and oregano are two herbs commonly used in the kitchen. They are closely related and quite easy to grow. If you enjoy fresh herbs for cooking, these are excellent additions to the landscape.

BOTANICAL INFO: *Herbaceous Perennial*

- Marjoram (*Origanum marjorana*)—hardy to zones 7–9
- Oregano (*Origanum vulgare*)—hardy to zones 5–9

GROWING GUIDE

Oregano is a Mediterranean herb so it doesn't like to get its feet wet, but it will tolerate poor soil. Marjoram prefers full sun as well. However, it will take some shade in the variegated plants. Most of these transplant well from plant starts. Sweet marjoram reseeds itself easily in the garden, but seedlings will often not breed true. ("Breeding true" means that plants grown from seeds resemble the parent plant.) Oregano can be seeded directly in the garden after temperatures reach 55 degrees.

Oregano and marjoram grow woody over time, so dig up the established clumps and divide them every few years. Pinching back the foliage and harvesting periodically helps keep the plant from becoming too leggy. For better harvests, keep the flower spikes trimmed to encourage more leaves. The flavor is more concentrated before the plant flowers. I'm usually more lax about this kind of maintenance, especially in an edible landscape, and do not mind the flowers.

POTENTIAL PESTS AND DISEASES

Very few pests and diseases.

HOW TO USE

Harvest the leaves before the flowers appear for the best flavor. However, I tend to use them fresh whenever I have them. Oregano has a substantive flavor and is commonly used in Italian and pasta dishes. Marjoram has sweeter varieties that aren't as pungent for eggs, salads, and dressings. Both can be dehydrated for use throughout the winter.

RECOMMENDATIONS

Sweet Marjoram or knotted marjoram grows about 2 feet tall and has attractive gray-green leaves. Italian marjoram (sometimes called Sicilian marjoram) is a hybrid of sweet marjoram and oregano and is very popular for cooking. Greek Oregano has spicy, full flavor and broader leaves. Aureum has golden-colored foliage that adds interest in the landscape. Compactum grows only a few inches tall but has a true spreading habit and is great for a rock garden or ground cover. Variegated forms are also available with white-edged foliage.

Oregano is a lovely herb for the garden. Photo courtesy of Alfred Diem.

Peppers are beautiful produce and ornamental in the landscape as well. Photo courtesy of Liz West.

☆ Peppers (*Capsicum* spp.)

Peppers are a must for warm-season edible landscapes because they have a beautiful shrub form and colorful ornamental fruit.

BOTANICAL INFORMATION: *Warm Season Annual (Perennial to zones 10–11)*

GROWING GUIDE

Peppers grow easily from seed. If you purchase seeds instead of already-started plants, you will have a much wider variety to choose from. Plant seeds in warm soil either indoors 6 weeks before your last frost date, or outdoors once the soil has warmed up. Peppers can take many weeks to mature, so starting them indoors is recommended and helpful.

Peppers need 12–18 inches of room to spread out. They can mix with other plants in a mixed border if you have space. One of my favorite ways to use them is to plant them in containers.

Water regularly for best flavor. Peppers are also fairly heavy feeders that will benefit from top dressing with compost and application of fertilizer a couple times a year. This is especially true if you have it planted in a container.

Peppers grow from 1–4 feet depending on the variety. They are generally divided into sweet peppers and hot peppers. Sweet peppers keep their mild flavor, even after they ripen. Hot peppers, on the other hand, range from mildly hot to extremely spicy.

POTENTIAL PESTS AND DISEASES

Aphids, flea beetles, and other pests like peppers. In fact, most of the same pests that trouble tomatoes also attack peppers.

HOW TO USE

Bell peppers or sweet peppers are amazing in a wide variety of dishes. They work in stir-fries, salads, and fajitas. I love grilling them and stuffing them also. Hot peppers are perfect for spicier dishes—salsa or hot sauce. Those are usually my husband's favorites. Plant a mix of sweet and hot so that you can enjoy both.

RECOMMENDATIONS

Sweet: Bullnose is a sweet pepper with delicious fruit perfect for salads. Thomas Jefferson grew it at Monticello. Chocolate Beauty is a large sweet pepper that ripens to a deep red-brown. Cherry Sweet produces 1-inch round red peppers that are also ornamental. King of the North ripens earlier than others in only 65–70 days. Lilac Bell produces large, eggplant-purple colored fruit. Italia is a sweet, long red pepper that looks like it might be spicy but isn't.

Hot: Anaheim is a popular, mildly flavored hot pepper that you can probably find as started plants in a garden nursery. Pretty in Purple is an ornamental pepper with burgundy and green variegated foliage and really attractive purple fruit that ripens yellow, orange, and scarlet. It's perfect for a stand-alone container. Fish Pepper is a curved, variegated green and white pepper that makes an excellent container plant. Golden Cayenne looks like a red cayenne pepper but ripens to a rich, golden yellow and is reported to be even spicier. Chinese Five Color is a super-hot pepper plant. It produces amazing peppers that ripen through multiple colors, turning from purple to cream to yellow to orange and finally to red when they are fully mature. Often you will see all five colors on the plant at one time.

Super Chili is a flavorful and ornamental hot pepper. Photo courtesy of All America Selections.

✿ Pot Marigold—*see Calendula in this chapter*

✿ Rhubarb (*Rheum rhabarbarum*)

Large leaves add a tropical flare to the landscape with very little maintenance required. A win-win for gardening ninjas.

BOTANICAL INFO: *Perennial*

Rhubarb is a cool-season vegetable hardy to zones 2–8.

GROWING GUIDE

Rhubarb plants have huge leaves on thick stalks that can easily reach 3–4 feet tall and 6 feet wide. The stalks are the edible part of the plant, but the leaves can add a mounding interest to the landscape in an area where lush growth would be appreciated. Since rhubarb require winter chill hours to develop thicker stems, southern zones should look for low-chill varieties.

Plant rhubarb divisions that contain at least one growing bud in the early fall and they will grow during the cool season. Late winter or spring harvests are possible.

Once you've harvested the rhubarb stalks, the plant will benefit from an application of fertilizer and mulch. Rhubarb typically does best when you allow the first year to be for establishing the root system. Plant them in full sun or provide them with part shade in warmer climates.

We don't always get a full two months of winter suitable for the chill requirements that rhubarb has. But if you have enough winter cool for rhubarb, the yummy stalks make a great early harvest.

POTENTIAL PESTS AND DISEASES

Some insects attack the leaves but not usually during the harvest period when things are cooler and milder.

Rhubarb leaves are broad and colorful, adding a lush, tropical feel to the garden. Photo courtesy of M. Williams, founder of A Moveable Garden.

HOW TO USE

DO NOT EAT THE LEAVES. Rhubarb stalks are the edible part of this plant. The leaves, even though they look like kale, are not edible. The stalks can be boiled, turned into pies, made into jam, and even wine.

RECOMMENDATIONS

Cherry Giant tolerates warmer climates and has reddish stalks. Victoria is a white stalk form.

❀ Rosemary (*Rosmarinus officinalis*)

This is one of my favorite herbs for edible landscaping.

BOTANICAL INFO: *Evergreen Shrubby Herb*

Hardy to zones 6–10 depending on conditions and varieties.

GROWING GUIDE

Rosemary can be grown from seed but takes two or more weeks to germinate. It takes several weeks after that to develop plants big enough to transplant out in the garden. It's much easier to start with plants already begun. Once rosemary gets well established and lays down its root system, it will be quite drought tolerant.

Rosemary's decorative, evergreen foliage combines well with other plants in the garden design. They can be grown as upright edges to a formal pathway or border or used as accent containers. Weeping forms will overlap the edges of raised beds and borders, or spill over containers beautifully.

Rosemary prefers neutral or slightly alkaline soil for best foliage and blooms. I love the traditional blue flowers but pink and white varieties also exist. Harvest year round whenever you need to use it, but never take more than ¼ of the stems at one time.

POTENTIAL PESTS AND DISEASES

No major pests or diseases.

Rosemary has pine needle–like foliage and beautiful blue flowers. Photo courtesy of Liz West.

HOW TO USE

Rosemary is such a fragrant, useful herb. In the kitchen, it's one of my favorites. It mixes well with many meat dishes, eggs, and vinegar dressings. It's amazing with potatoes too. I love using rosemary stems as shish kababs on the grill for roasting veggies and stuff too.

RECOMMENDATIONS

Arp is a semi-upright 4–5 feet tall variety with pale blue flowers and cold hardy to zone 6. Santa Rosa Trailing is one of my favorites because its weeping habit will drape over containers and raised bed edges beautifully. Tuscan Blue is a huge shrub growing up to 7 feet tall—a great choice for grill skewers. Golden Rain grows only 3–4 feet tall and has yellow-tinged foliage on its new growth. White Rosemary has white flowers growing about 4 feet tall. Pink Rosemary is a name given to a couple different types of pink blooming rosemaries. The one I have has a slight weeping habit. Salem is a dwarf form that grows only 2 feet tall. It's nice for edges and formal borders.

☆ Sage (*Salvia officinalis*)

So useful in the garden as well as the kitchen, this common culinary herb is a rock star in the edible landscape.

BOTANICAL INFORMATION:
Shrubby Perennial

Hardy to zones 4–10.

GROWING GUIDE

Starting from seeds will delay your harvest for a year, so I tend to purchase plants already started. Sage transplants well and can be planted directly where you want it in the garden. Grow sage in full sun or part shade in medium-rich soil for the best growth, but it will tolerate less-than-ideal conditions. Just give them well-draining soil and don't overwater.

Golden variegated sage contrasts beautifully with prostrating rosemary in this herb container planter.

Harvesting from the growing tips will encourage good growth. The plant will tend toward leggy, woody growth if it isn't cut back from time to time. As with most herbs, the strongest flavor comes from harvesting leaves before the flower spikes begin. Not all cultivars produce flowers but sage that produces flowers attract bees, butterflies, and hummingbirds.

POTENTIAL PESTS AND DISEASES

Root rot is a problem in moist soil conditions. In humid areas or if the plants are overcrowded, fungal infections can be a problem.

HOW TO USE

Sage is used all the time in the kitchen, especially in meat dishes. It's a common seasoning for sausages and stuffings. It's also great in baked potatoes and Italian dishes.

RECOMMENDATIONS

Pineapple sage has a fruity overtone that is great for lighter dishes. Icterina is a golden-green and dark-green variegated sage. Tri-color is one of my favorite variegated sage plants because of its gray, purple, and green leaves. Holt's Mammoth has leaves nearly 5 inches long. Red Sage or Purpurascens has red-violet new growth that later deepens into the traditional gray-green.

✿ Sunflowers (*Helianthus annuus*)

Sunflowers are so cheerful and add amazing blooms in the summer and fall landscape. Not every variety produces edible seeds.

BOTANICAL INFORMATION: *Annual*

GROWING GUIDE

Sunflowers are easy to grow. The large seeds make them easy to plant, especially for kids. Pollenless sunflowers do not set seed, but the ones that produce seeds will attract birds to the garden.

Check the days to maturity information on the sunflower seed packet descriptions and plant sunflowers with different maturity times to extend your harvest. Sunflowers will grow anywhere from 18 inches to 10 feet tall.

POTENTIAL PESTS AND DISEASES

Birds are the biggest pests for sunflowers and will take all your seed harvest, if you let them.

HOW TO USE

Sunflowers can have blooms nearly a foot wide. Stunning! Photo courtesy of Jeannie Sanders.

Sunflower seeds are bland when they are freshly harvested. To prepare them more like those in the store, you can salt and roast them. Sunflower seeds have great oils with good fats, and they are excellent to add to salads as good source of protein.

RECOMMENDATIONS

Mammoth is one of the best giant forms and will grow easily 8–10 feet tall at the minimum. Sunspot grows much shorter, about 2 feet tall but still has full-sized blooms that produce seeds. Autumn Beauty has gorgeous 6-inch wide flowers in a mix of burgundy, rust, and gold. Evening Sun grows 7 feet tall and has medium-large flowers with yellow, rust, and crimson. My favorites in this mix are the bicolored sunflowers. Italian White grows smaller flowers, creamy colored, with a dark rust-brown center. Red Sun has branching plants that reach 5–6 feet tall. While the tiny seeds aren't as good for eating, they are loved by birds.

☆ Swiss Chard (*Beta vulgaris*)

Swiss chard is an amazing vegetable that isn't grown nearly often enough in the garden. And to top it all off, it's gorgeous in the landscape!

BOTANICAL INFORMATION: *Biennial, but grown as an Annual*

GROWING GUIDE

Swiss chard grows easily from seed. The seeds resemble beet seeds; they are large and easy to plant. Swiss chard grows rapidly and is harvested in its first year.

Swiss chard has broad leaves with colorful stalks and veins. It doesn't bolt to seed as quickly as other greens. We've found it remarkably heat tolerant in our tough summer areas. I also appreciate that you can eat both stalk and leaves from this plant.

The main thing with Swiss chard is to keep the plants evenly watered. A good mulch of compost and straw keeps them from drying out and turning bitter. Swiss chard tastes best when it's able to grow well without drought or poor periods.

POTENTIAL PESTS AND DISEASES

Snails and slugs are sometimes a problem for Swiss chard. Aphids can be a problem as well, less so in a fall garden than in the spring.

HOW TO USE

Swiss chard leaves can be used as a replacement for lettuce in salads or as a replacement for spinach when it's cooked. The stalks have the texture of celery but the taste is closer to asparagus in flavor. I love to sauté them lightly with butter and garlic, or drizzle them with oil and sea salt and roast them in the oven.

Swiss chard comes with a variety of brightly colored stalks and veins. Photo courtesy of Jeannie Sanders.

RECOMMENDATIONS

Bright Lights is sometimes called Five Color or Rainbow. It produces stems in a variety of colors, including red, pink, yellow, orange, and white. It's an All-America Selection winner for good reason. Ruby or Ruby Red has crimson stalks with heavily wrinkled leaves. It may bolt after frost, but the beauty is so worth it. Charlotte has cherry-red stalks and dark-green foliage. Flamingo Pink has nearly neon-pink stalks that are gorgeous in the garden for bright pops of color.

☆ Violas/Violets (*Viola* spp.)

Violets, violas, and pansies are all in the viola family. In addition to being one of the prettiest flowers in my cottage garden patch, they are also edible.

BOTANICAL INFO: *Cool Season Perennials*

- Viola (*Viola cornuta*)
- Johnny Jump-Ups (*Viola tricolor*)
- Violet (*Viola odorata*)—hardy to zones 4–9
- Pansy (*Viola x. wittrockiana*)

GROWING GUIDE

Sow seeds directly in the garden in the fall, or start plants indoors and transplant in the spring. If you aren't sure what specific cultivar you want, browse the selections available at your local garden nursery where you have a chance to view the plants flower color and growth habit. Once they are growing happily in your garden, they are very likely to reseed themselves year after year.

Violets and violas tend to be much smaller plants, sometimes as small as 3–4 inches tall. Pansies can grow much larger and have larger flowers as well. While plants in this family tend to favor full sun, they do not tolerate high heat levels. In my area, they are better suited for dappled and part shade areas and seem to naturalize well there as a bright-light understory level plant. Water and mulch helps them withstand the heat of summer.

These violets make themselves at home in the crevices of the cool, rock steps in this garden. Photo courtesy of Liz West.

I love these perennial flowers, even though the season I get to enjoy them is rather small. The foliage forms pleasing clumps and the leaves are often semi-heart shaped. The flowers are colorful, charming, and abundant. They also look like cheerful faces. All the plants in the viola family has a lot of purple variations available but they are also available in yellow, white, orange, and many bicolor and tricolor effects.

I love these classically colored Johnny Jump-Ups used as edging plants in this mixed herb border. Photo courtesy of Patrick Standish.

POTENTIAL PESTS AND DISEASES

Powdery mildew can be a problem for some of these plants, especially if they are overcrowded. Slugs and snails can be a problem, especially in humid climates.

HOW TO USE

Violas, violets, and pansies all have edible flowers. The petals of violas and pansies taste a bit like lettuce when added to salads. They can also be used in vinegar and oil infusions, candied for topping desserts and cakes, and even made into jellies or syrup. Violets, on the other hand, have a sweeter taste that is definitely floral tasting and is a favorite for sugaring to add to cakes and desserts. It's also great used plain in teas, beverages, salads, and garnishes for other dishes.

RECOMMENDATIONS

With violets, the more fragrant varieties will often have the strongest flavor. Some violas and pansies are also fragrant, but not all.

Pansies: Swiss Giant mixes are excellent pansies and available in a variety of colors. Orange Sun is a bright apricot-orange color. Bowle's Black is a stunning dark-purple that looks black, especially in the shade. Pansiolas are a hybrid between violas and pansies developed by Proven Winners. I love Sugarplum, which has deep purple, light purple, and white centered petals.

Viola: Etain is a classic viola that blooms longer than average and has gorgeous cream-yellow flowers with purple edges. It's one of my favorites. Silver Gem has silvery leaves and purple flowers, making an interesting ground cover for shade. Rebecca has white flowers with purple edges and streaks throughout.

Violets: Parma Comte de Brazza is a rare white blooming violet that has ruffled petals. Sweet Rosina is a pink-purple violet with old-fashioned shape and sweet fragrance. The Czar has single deep-purple flowers that are highly fragrant.

Edible Landscaping is simply a matter of putting the right plants in the right spaces. The possibilities and combinations are nearly endless. This book focused on edible-only designs to help show you what can be done, but edibles can be tucked in with ornamentals as well. You now have all the tools you need to assess your home, plan garden spaces, and select amazing plants that give you the best of both worlds—edible and ornamental. You have everything you need to garden like a ninja. If you want to show off what you're doing or join a group where you can ask specific questions, please come join the community at http://UntrainedHousewife.com/GardeningLikeANinja. I love seeing what gardeners are doing with their unique situations.

Resources

There are so many gardening companies and products out there that it can feel very overwhelming when you are starting out. Below you'll find some of the resources shown or discussed in this book, as well as others I personally like. But resources can change. To see an always-updated link of gardening resources, visit http://UntrainedHousewife.com/EdibleLandscapingResources.

WEBSITES TO CONNECT WITH AND GET MORE INFORMATION FROM ME

- **Untrained Housewife: Gardening Like a Ninja course and downloads.**
  http://UntrainedHousewife.com/GardeningLikeANinja

- **Facebook Group about Edible Landscaping** — Connect with a community of fellow edible landscapers. https://www.facebook.com/groups/EdibleLandscapingGuide/

- **Garden Journal Free Printables** — Free to download and print off as needed.
  http://BackyardFarmingGuide.com

GARDEN NURSERIES AND SEED COMPANIES FOR QUALITY PLANTS

- **Baker Creek Seeds** — A huge selection of heirloom seeds from all over the world. Unique varieties available. Very limited number of started plants.

  http://www.rareseeds.com/

  2278 Baker Creek Road
  Mansfield, MO 65704
  417-924-8917
  seeds@rareseeds.com

- **Swallowtail Garden Seeds** — Over 1,500 vegetable, annual, perennial, and herb seeds.

  http://www.swallowtailgardenseeds.com/

  122 Calistoga Road, #178
  Santa Rosa, CA 95409
  1-877-489-7333 or 707-538-3585
  info@swallowtailgardenseeds.com

- **Peaceful Valley Grow Organic** — Many organic seeds, soil supplements, plants, and tools.

    https://www.groworganic.com/

    125 Clydesdale Court
    Grass Valley, CA 95945
    530-272-4769
    helpdesk@groworganic.com

- **Renee's Garden Seeds** — Small seed company with unique annuals, perennials, and easy-to-grow-from-seed herbs and vegetables.

    http://www.reneesgarden.com/

    6060 Graham Hill Rd.
    Felton, CA 95018
    888-880-7228
    customerservice@reneesgarden.com

- **Old House Gardens** — Unique, heirloom bulbs that are difficult to find anywhere else.

    https://www.oldhousegardens.com/

    536 Third St.,
    Ann Arbor, MI 48103
    (734) 995-1486
    help@oldhousegardens.com

- **Nature Hills Nursery** — Large selection of trees, shrubs, and perennials.

    http://www.naturehills.com/

    9910 N. 48th Street, Suite 200
    Omaha, NE 68152
    888-864-7663
    info@naturehills.com

- **Raintree Nursery** — Wide selection of herbs, fruit, vines, ornamentals, and unusual edibles.

    http://www.raintreenursery.com/

    391 Butts Rd.
    Morton, WA 98356
    (360) 496-6400
    customerservice@raintreenursery.com

- **Proven Winners** — Plant hybridizers and developers with unique cultivars of annuals, perennials, and shrubs.

  https://www.provenwinners.com/

  111 E Elm St Ste D
  Sycamore, IL 60178
  815-895-8130

- **All-America Selections** — Dedicated to trialing and promoting new seed varieties.

  http://all-americaselections.org/

  1311 Butterfield Road, Suite 310
  Downers Grove, IL 60515-5625
  Phone: 630-963-0770

- **Bailey Nurseries** — Many perennials, shrubs, and trees both ornamental and edible.

  https://www.baileynurseries.com/

  1325 Bailey Road
  St. Paul, MN 55119
  651-768-3412
  ryan.mcenaney@baileynurseries.com

CONTAINERS, TOOLS, AND HARDSCAPING ELEMENTS

- **Fiskars** — Wide variety of tools for yard work and gardening maintenance.
  http://www2.fiskars.com/Products/Gardening-and-Yard-Care

- **Corona Tools** — High quality tools for gardening, pruning, and more.
  http://coronatoolsusa.com/

  (800) 847-7863

- **Vita Gardens** — Raised bed, keyhole, and accessibility planters for small-space garden.
  http://www.vitagardens.com/

  211 Campbell St.
  Sarnia, ON Canada
  N7T 2G9
  Phone: 800-282-9346
  eddie@vitagardens.com

- **Side Planting Containers** — The containers that Pamela Crawford uses for her beautiful containers, many of which are featured in this book.
  http://www.sideplanting.com/
  http://www.kinsmangarden.com/category/Container-Gardening

- **Pottery Express** — The glazed and Mexican containers featured in some of the photos in this book and in my original garden designs.
  http://potteryexpress.com/

  25370 Zemel Rd
  Punta Gorda, FL 33955
  (941) 505-8400
  ContactUs@PotteryExpress.com

 About the Author

A mother of five living in rural Oklahoma with her husband, Angela is the founder of Untrained Housewife, cofounder of the Homestead Bloggers Network, and expert for Organic Gardening at About.com. She is the author of *Backyard Farming on an Acre (More or Less)* (Alpha Books, 2013), as well as several other books, all with the common theme of helping people embrace the journey. When she's able to get away from home, it's usually to speak at a blog conference. She loves empowering others with whatever is the next step on their self-sufficiency journey. But don't stress about perfection—Angela calls herself a get-it-done-ist, not a purist, and connects with you at whatever level you're starting from. Join her on Twitter at @AngEngland or pop into the Edible Landscaping Guide Facebook group.

SCAN TO VISIT

WWW.UNTRAINEDHOUSEWIFE.COM